FIERCE

FIERCE

Women of the Bible and
Their Stories of Violence,
Mercy, Bravery, Wisdom,
Sex, and Salvation

·
·
·
·
·
·
·

ALICE CONNOR

Fortress Press
Minneapolis

FIERCE
Women of the Bible and Their Stories of Violence, Mercy, Bravery, Wisdom, Sex, and Salvation

Illustrator: Leighton Connor

Cover design: Brad Norr

Print ISBN: 978-1-5064-1070-8
eBook ISBN: 978-1-5064-1071-5

Manufactured in the U.S.A.

To my great-great-great-grandmother Ellen,
who begat Alice C,
who begat Alice T,
who begat Marjorie,
who begat Nancye,
who begat me.

That *woman* was the first word spoken
must have taken even the angels by surprise,
who were used to bringing their fiery glory
down to the clanging swords of battlefields,
to priests tugging at their beards
in lamentation, to voices thundering in temples
and muscles hefting stones from mountaintops,
not to a trembling woman whose hair clung
to her neck with tears, who for a moment
held the souls of the nations like a basket of figs.

—TANIA RUNYAN, "THE EMPTY TOMB"

Paradoxically, human love is sanctified not in the height of attraction and enthusiasm but in the everyday struggles of living with another person. It is not in romance but in routine that the possibilities for transformation are made manifest. And that requires commitment.

—KATHLEEN NORRIS, *THE QUOTIDIAN MYSTERIES: LAUNDRY, LITURGY, AND "WOMEN'S WORK"*

KID: H-how'd you do that?
BUFFY: It's what I do.
KID: But you're . . . you're just a girl.
BUFFY: That's what *I* keep saying.

—AFTER BUFFY HANDILY DEFEATS A VAMPIRE, "THE GIFT,"
BUFFY THE VAMPIRE SLAYER, 2001

Contents

Part 3. Christian Women

Introduction: Together with Certain Women

Years ago, I was chaplain at outdoor adventure camp. That first year wasn't particularly adventuresome: we stayed in the air-conditioned cabins and learned to tie knots. In later years, we set up tents in the woods, made our own food, chopped our own wood, and brushed our teeth over an open pit. It being a Christian summer camp, we led spiritual exercises based on God's fingerprints on the natural world. We trekked through the woods, our skin coated with a constant slime of bug spray, and talked about exodus and foraging and God's provision of manna in the desert. We lay in the grass and speculated about how we're made of dirt and how, in a pervasive and self-hating way, we think we're dirty. We wrote down our sins and buried them in the dirt, and then the counselors and I planted daisies on top of each of burial plot for the campers to find in the morning. It's summer camp; it's kind of required to do cheesy-but-meaningful activities. Don't judge.

The last year I worked outdoor adventure, I was enormously pregnant with my daughter—like, so pregnant that when people walking behind me saw me turn around, they gasped and said, "Whoa." I was not about to subject my lumbering self to a dubious air mattress, so I stayed just over the hill in the retreat center. Air-conditioning and a real bed: sign me up. One afternoon, I was down at the camp, sitting in one of those folding camp chairs, which are meant to be comfortable but really, really aren't. As I sat there, I watched campers and counselors chopping wood. It's hard work, chopping wood. Even watching it made me tired. I said to the counselor nearby, "You know, in American pioneer days, pregnant women had to chop the wood, start the fires, cook the food, wash the clothes, fight off scavengers, and care for the other children. And I can barely stand up to get a cookie from the storage bins over there. Those pioneer women were damned fierce. And probably exhausted." She felt my logic was sound, and we decided to form the Women's Pioneer League; the only requirement for membership was a deep awe for the women who'd gone before us and all they'd accomplished, pregnant or not.

I've been in awe of the women who have gone before me ever since I could comprehend their stories. My great-aunts—there were six of them—lived in a house that used to be a speakeasy. For years after they moved in, men would come to the back door, asking for bathtub liquor. My great-aunts worked during World War II in a factory that made sanitary napkins. And that's all I know about them. They didn't think their stories were worth retelling, so we don't know them.

My daughter—the one who filled my belly that summer at camp—is now seven and is a fierce little girl. She throws tantrums when she's interrupted and protects her little brother from real and imagined threats. She knows that anyone can love anyone and verbally pushes back when her friends say otherwise. She wants to be a school principal, a sign-language interpreter, and an artist when she grows up. She rolls her eyes when I talk to her about our trans friends and not assuming anything about other people's gender. "I *know*, Mama," she says. With her daddy, she created a digital comic about a warrior princess who was raised by unicorns in a post-apocalyptic world, defeats bad guys, and helps turn the electricity back on (shameless plug: electricteamcomic.com).

I worry that she will grow up never having really heard about all the fierce women in her life and in the Bible. Because we adult women have a hard time telling our own stories and articulating what we've learned from them about God and transcendence. Because we don't read or talk about women in the Bible much in church, and the Bible itself tends to skate right over them anyway. When women do show up, they seem to be players in a man's story. Or they're victims of violence whose victimhood teaches the nation a lesson. Or the church offers their stories as morality tales about how to be better wives and mothers. There are already a hundred books about women in the Bible trying to teach us just that, and bless their hearts, so many of them are condescending or even downright offensive. Look, I'm a wife and a mother, and I can always try to be better at both of them. I'm the world's okayest mom—I've got a mug and everything. But I'm not just a mother and a wife; I'm also a fiber artist and an Enneagram enthusiast and a science-fiction reader and a gardener and a citizen of democracy and a neighbor and a friend and a daughter of aging parents.

I am also an Episcopal priest and the daughter of a priest, so I'm an insider to the church. I can define realized eschatology, and I know how to properly use an aspergillum. I know my privileges of whiteness, middle-classness, educatedness, and presumed straightness. But I've always felt like an outsider. There were the consistently good grades when it was the height of uncool to be a smart chick. And the feeling of superiority I wrapped around myself as protection against anti-intellectual teasing. There was the grunge era, when my high school had not yet discovered Nirvana, so my flea market combat boots and fishnet stockings were laughed at. There was the time in junior high school when I was walking home from school and a boy walking by thought it'd be fine to pinch my ass. There was the advocating for gay rights with my conservative, southern high school peers. And then there's the feeling of alienation from the scripture of my own church.

I loved the church. I grew up in the Episcopal Church and loved the pomp and circumstance of weekly worship. I loved singing hymns in four-part harmony in the church choir (and being the only teenager in a group of retirees). I loved arguing theology with my father at the dinner table. I loved knowing the order of the books of the Bible. But at the same time, I never knew what to do with the women in that Bible. They were problems. And *I* was a problem. One Sunday when I mentioned in the choir room that I thought we ought to be praying for the young man who'd been in the news for killing his wife, one of the older men angrily shut me down, saying that such a person wasn't worth praying for. It felt like he was saying there was something wrong with me for wanting to. But didn't Jesus say to pray for our enemies? Aren't the least and smallest and youngest supposed to be the ones God chooses? Did I get it wrong? Is there something wrong with *me*? I didn't know what to do with my *self*.

The story I've heard about women in the Bible, whether accidentally or on purpose, is about victims and tempters and silence. Sometimes we read between the lines to understand a story better, but much of the time, it's all right there, and we just forgot.

Just as you and I are not two-dimensional, so the women in the Bible aren't either. There are many ways to hear and connect with their stories. There are multiple right answers to the questions they ask of us. I try to see their stories through lenses of slavery, poverty, disaster, sexual minority, and disability, as well as discovery, connection, and joy. Anything I come away from them with is only a partial truth. Yet for thousands of years, we have *heard* only partial truths about them.

There's so much more.

In the beginning of the book of Acts, after Judas's suicide and Jesus' inexplicable floating off into the clouds, the disciples were lost. The surviving male disciples, "together with certain women," went to an upstairs room to pray. Who were these certain women implied to be in the inner circle of grief and new purpose? Who else was there and helped choose a new disciple to take Judas's place? Mary of Magdala, Mary Jesus' mom, the Other Mary (it was a popular name)? And Certain Women are peppered throughout scripture, present at key moments, saying the things the men couldn't or wouldn't, doing things that earned men praise but women dismissal.

What happened to these stories? What happened to these women with their stories of neglect or celebration, anger or mercy? What, for that matter, has happened to the stories of our own mothers and grandmothers and great-grandmothers? We are all part of the story that God is telling. We all—regardless of gender identity—can be as fierce as our great-grandmothers and Tamar and all the Marys. Sometimes our ferocity is almost invisible, but it is not extinguished. When we read their stories, we can see not only their particular, fearsome lives but also our own.

It's not just women who need to rediscover our stories. There's a pervasive misunderstanding, on the Internet at least, that stories about women are just for women, but that stories about men are for all people—are universal. Feminism gets derided as a two-dimensional, categorical rejection of men. Perhaps out of an understandable fear of change, feminism isn't allowed to be multifaceted or to encourage all people to find their voices and use them. In reality, it's about recognizing our common humanity—men, women, transpeople, everyone—and not just allowing but delighting in stories where women do awesome things (I'm looking at you, *Mad Max: Fury Road*). It's not about taking anything away from men.

When we talk about feminism in the church, in the workplace, and in our families, these conversations are all about power: who has it, who doesn't have it, what it's used for. These are good questions to ask, don't get me wrong. But as Christians, we are called to something else. The God we worship, the God made human, seems to be all about the power*less*, the outsider, whatever that means in a given story. And so often in our scripture, God calls us not to success but to faithfulness. God calls us not to power but to presence.

So here's the plan: Each chapter in this book is a retelling of a woman's story recorded in the Jewish or Christian Bible (that means the Old and New Testaments). The stories are told in different ways as they inspired me. They're meant to be a bit complex, maybe a bit ambiguous, and to spark some memory of your own. How are you like Susanna or Asherah or Phoebe? The chapters are grouped into three sections. The first, titled "The Only Four (plus Mary)," is about the four women listed in Jesus' genealogy in Matthew's gospel (plus Mary who isn't technically related to any of them). "Hebrew Women" is about women in the Old Testament; "Christian Women" is about women in the New Testament. At the end of the book, you'll find a list of Bible references for each chapter so you can read these stories yourself, followed by a short list of resources for further reading. There are probably twenty-seven thousand other books and articles you could read about any of these women, so I listed ones I found particularly intriguing or challenging.

Additionally, at fierceasswomen.com, you can find questions to help you go deeper in your exploration of these our foremothers, as well as Pinterest boards, and other resources.

The stories present in our Bible are messy and challenging and beautiful. This book is meant, honestly, to provoke you, to open up possibilities for you, to invite you to imagine the inner lives of other women, and even to offend at times, as the prophets did. It's meant to help you see how similar you are to these women who are so far from us in years and so close to us in their desires and abilities. It is meant for women and men and teenagers and retirees and anyone ready to argue with scripture, as the woman at the well argued with Jesus. The truths I offer in this book are not the whole truth, but they'll help us in our wrestling.

The Only Four (plus Mary)

One of the best sermons I ever heard was about the genealogy of Jesus in the first chapter of Matthew. Weird, right? It's the passage you are thinking of with all the "begats." Who preaches on that? A preacher who, it turns out, I'd had an intense, unrequited crush on in college, that's who.

Years after I got over that crush, I went to a Christmas Eve service with my new husband's family. It was a charming Protestant church in eastern Kentucky with the pews set up in arcs around the central dais, the full-immersion baptismal swimming pool behind the altar. The preacher, my old crush, spoke about how he was new to the congregation and was still trying to figure out how everyone was related—or, as we say in Kentucky, how you're kin. He spoke about the expectations we have of folks we're kin to, how we view some folks in the family based on who else they're kin to, and what it means to be in a family together. He said he'd always thought Jesus—mighty God, the Everlasting Father, the Prince of Peace—would be kin to all kinds of faithful, righteous folk, that his perfection would be reflected in his family tree. About that: Jesus' family is full of murderers and adulterers and just difficult people. I can relate.

What I find fascinating about Jesus' kin in that long, boring "begat" passage is the four women who are listed. Of the forty generations named in that list, only four people are women: Tamar the Trickster, Rahab the Prostitute, Bathsheba the wife of Uriah, and Ruth the Filthy Foreigner. Plus, at the end, there's Mary the mother of Jesus, not actually related to any of the other people. What an odd collection. Scholars have written heaps of articles about why these four and what they have in common besides, you know, being in the genealogy. They're all outsiders to the Jewish people, who prided themselves on their clear national boundaries. Their sexuality is a huge part of their stories in a culture where women's bodies were not valued. They were important enough, interesting enough, maybe difficult enough to merit Matthew's mentioning them alongside all the other difficult kin.

So thanks, Former Crush, for bringing them to my attention.

Tamar

When Sleeping with Your Father-in-Law Is Righteous

> As she was being brought out, she sent word to her father-in-law, "It was the owner of these who made me pregnant." And she said, "Take note, please, whose these are, the signet and the cord and the staff." Then Judah acknowledged them and said, "She is more in the right than I, since I did not give her to my son Shelah." And he did not lie with her again.
>
> —GENESIS 38:25–26

I'm not going to lie to you: Tamar is a bad-ass. It's not like you'd know it, since we don't ever read about her in church. There aren't any charming nursery wallpapers or knitting patterns depicting her Bible story. And honestly, the story is awkward for modern audiences. For all I know, it was awkward back in the day as well.

Tamar lived in Canaan, the area of the ancient Middle East that was both delightfully verdant and populated with filthy, sexually threatening Canaanites. Later it was called the Promised Land and even later the nation of Israel. Canaan was more of a region than a country, and all kinds of folks lived there, including Jews. I'm telling you all this because the word *Canaan* is heavy with meaning. It was the country that the Israelites entered after

11

wandering in the desert for forty years and that apparently flowed with milk and honey. Canaan was both the destination that was longed for during the exodus and a catchall word for foreigners who good Jews could not mix with (here, "mix with" means to have sex and children with). Canaan was a liminal space—that is, a place of transition where multiple experiences are true simultaneously. Like I said, awkward. This is where Tamar was from; these were her kin.

Judah, our other main character, was one of Joseph's brothers. You remember Joseph: he got the Technicolor dream coat and interpreted dreams and was a little bit of an ass to his brothers. Judah was the oldest of the brothers and had settled down with his family in Canaan, in the region of the Adullamites. The Adullamites were all right in his book, so he negotiated for his eldest son, Er, to marry one of them, Tamar. It's too bad Er has fallen out of popularity in baby name books, but it turns out he was wicked in the sight of the Lord, so maybe it's for the best. We don't know the details of his wickedness, but it was bad enough that God killed him—just dropped him right there, like it was nothing. Poor Tamar, to have her husband die so quickly. It's not that she loved him passionately, the way you might read in a romance novel ("Her breath came quickly now at the touch of his hand on hers; she'd never had such a strong physical response to a man before . . ."). No, even though she was property and part of a legal transaction, Tamar might have grown to care for Er, as her mother did for her father. They might have had a mutually fulfilling partnership. Or maybe not, what with his wickedness in the sight of the Lord.

Never fear, though: Judah's family practiced levirate marriage, which meant that if a man died, his next-oldest brother would marry the wife, and their future children would be raised as the children of the dead brother. It was a kind of creepy way to carry on a family name, but that sort of thing was important then. It still is, come to that. So Tamar was married off to Er's brother Onan. "Okay," she might have thought, "I knew this was a possibility. Onan is a good man. Let's do this." But Onan, it seems, was also wicked in the sight of the Lord; only this time, we know what he did. Because he didn't care for levirate marriage and wanted his kids to have *his* name, when he had sex with Tamar, he practiced coitus interruptus. He ejaculated onto the ground so Tamar wouldn't get pregnant. So, of course, God killed him, too. Poor Tamar, to have her second husband die so quickly. Tamar might have thought, "Are you kidding me? And still no kids. What the hell?"

Fun fact: The church for centuries used this story as a warning not to masturbate, but that really isn't what's going on here. The science of the time said that semen, rather than containing half of the genetic code for a person, was basically tiny, complete babies that would be implanted in the woman, who was just an incubator. So Onan's sin was wasting human lives. It was also disobedience to authority—kind of a theme in the Bible, beginning with Eve and Adam.

Never fear, though: Judah had a third son, Shelah. He was still too young to marry, so Judah sent Tamar back to her family, promising to wed her to Shelah when he was old enough. It was a thin excuse. Judah feared for his son's life if he married him to this black widow. His two sons' deaths couldn't have been their fault; they were upright members of the family, so obviously she was doing something to them. Best to send her away. Now, it's pivotal to know that at the time, women's only worth was in producing children—male children in particular. Women went from being part of their father's household to part of their husband's household. To be part of neither was a singular shame and a perplexing space. Tamar was no longer her father's property or her husband's, nor was she yet Shelah's wife. She was in a liminal space among the three. Poor Tamar, to be sent home in disgrace—a woman without a home, powerless.

Later—years later, it seems, since Shelah was now old enough to marry but had not yet taken Tamar—Judah's wife died. He took his Adullamite friend and went out into the pastures to work with his sheep again. Maybe he'd been caught up in caring for his wife over a long illness, or maybe he just needed to work off his grief by shearing and milking, but this was a new thing, going to the pastures. He had to travel a ways to get there.

Tamar heard of her mother-in-law's death, of Judah's new-found passion for shearing and milking, and of course, she observed that she had not yet been married to Shelah. He was long since old enough to marry. What was the holdup? Tamar was sitting home, every day falling deeper and deeper into disgrace, stared at as she walked from one part of the camp to another, whispered about with pity and knowing glances. And there was Judah heading out to get his own life going again while Tamar's was dying on the vine.

"So that's how it is," she thought. Simmering with the injustice of it, her brain going over the possibilities, she decided to take back what was hers. Poor Tamar no longer, she took off her widow's weeds and dressed herself up with jewelry and her finest clothing and covered her face with a veil. No one would recognize her this way. She hurried ahead to the gate at Enaim, a transition point between the land of the Adullamites and the next region over—a kind of border crossing. She sat at the gate, waiting for her father-in-law, her plan taking shape.

Judah, out of breath from walking far from his home and ready for an overnight stop, saw Tamar sitting at the gate. He saw her, and he wanted her. Obviously she was a prostitute; who else would sit at the gate with her face covered? He was tired, he was in mourning, and he had money. Why not hire her to warm his bed that night? Realizing that he, in fact, did not have money with him, he offered her a baby goat in payment to be sent on later—like, "Baby, I'll get you an iPhone after we get it on." Tamar was not stupid and asked for collateral on his payment: his signet, cord, and staff—his identification, irreplaceable. He trusted this "prostitute" he'd just met, and he willingly turned them over and followed her to bed.

There is no description of their sexy times, no Song of Songs–style "midsections like ivory," no uncovering of feet or thighs. It happened between sentences. Was it a quick-and-dirty transaction? Did they both get what they wanted but not really? Afterward, she changed her clothes back to her widow's weeds and returned home, ready to play the long game. Judah sent his Adullamite friend back to the town where he'd met her with the baby goat, but comically, the townspeople say in unison, "There ain't never been a prostitute at the gate. Nope, not a one." Judah had to go home without making a fuss, because it was embarrassing. He'd trusted this stranger, he'd lost his identification, and they couldn't even find one lousy prostitute. Just hush it up; it's fine, it'll be fine.

Of course, it was not fine. Three weeks later, Tamar was pregnant, and word got back to Judah: "Guess who's knocked up? Your daughter-in-law who couldn't get pregnant with your first two sons, who died under mysterious circumstances! Mazel tov!" Judah was pissed and ordered her to be burned alive for her treachery. Tamar, with ovaries of steel, calmly said she knew who the father of the child was and wouldn't you like to know, dearest father-in-law? She said, "I've got his signet, cord, and staff right here, and as we all know, those can't be faked with today's technology. You'll know for sure who knocked me up if you see them." Judah, full of his superior indignation, said, "Bring them out. He, too, will burn!"

Oh, son, wrong answer. "Take note whose these are," she said, probably with a saucy glint in her eye, thinking, "Don't mess with me, fellas." His eyes fell on his own signet, cord, and staff, which he'd believed lost forever to the disappearing prostitute of Enaim, and everyone gasped. It was like an ancient episode of Maury Povich: "You are the father."

You'd think he'd go into a rage, have her killed anyway, and be lauded for ridding their community of such a threatening and unhinged woman. Amazingly, he affirmed that he was the father and then, making everyone's jaw drop, said she was more righteous than he. He had not done right by his daughter-in-law, so she was right in her devious plan. Intentionally sleeping with your father-in-law to trap him in his lies is more righteous than protecting your third son from possible death. Interesting.

If you're like me, you're thinking, "You show him, Tamar!" and also "What am I supposed to do with this?" at the same time. It's weird to see an incestuous, extramarital affair held up as a good thing. God, it would seem, is about mess and dark comedy as much as righteousness and stability. Being a wife and mother was Tamar's right, so she retrieved it from Judah with the means she had, however unsavory. It was her job to stand up for herself. Tamar's actions are justified by the genealogy writers, who listed her in the lineage of King David as having had sons *by Judah.* That one-night stand made possible King David and, eventually, Jesus son of Mary.

Tamar is what we call a trickster, a character in folklore around the world who breaks rules, turns culture on its head, and uses deception to show truth. Tricksters often work in selfish ways, but their tricks reveal the dishonesty of others. Tricksters show us that things don't have to be the way they've always been, that the way things are—whatever that is to you in your time and place—is changeable. You know what they're doing is wrong on some level, but it's also deliciously right and so hilarious and awkward that you can't look away.

Tricksters are considered heroes. Think about Bugs Bunny or Anansi from West Africa or Loki in Nordic myth. Think about Abraham, who twice passed off his wife Sarah as his sister, "accidentally" sold her to kings, and became wealthy himself. Think of Judith, who fooled her enemy Holofernes into thinking she loved him before cutting off his head and saving her people. Think of Jacob, who cheated everyone he came into contact with and was the namesake of the Israelite people. Even then, folks knew that the system didn't work, that it ended up hurting the very people it's supposed to help. Sometimes the system, the culture, needs to take itself less seriously.

Tamar reminds me that the systems we live in are still unjust and secretive, and sometimes they need to be tricked to reveal themselves. Edward Snowden is a modern trickster. He leaked thousands of documents showing massive surveillance and privacy violation by the United States government. He is a traitor to country but a hero to humanity—a person between truths, like Tamar.

You may not have heard of Alexandra Elbakyan, a Kazakhstani researcher. She created a website called Sci-Hub, which evades the paywalls on all online scientific publishing and archival sites, allowing researchers free access to a huge amount of necessary information. That may seem like piracy—actually, it is; it is piracy. But it's important to know that the researchers whose work is published on those sites are not paid for their work, and the fees to access the information are so exorbitant that even institutions like Harvard have canceled their subscriptions. Alexandra Elbakyan is a modern trickster, creating a clearly illegal tool to reform an exploitative system. She, too, is a woman between truths.

Tamar the Trickster says, "Things are not as they should be; things are not as God dreams them to be." I'm not much of a trickster myself. My husband is constantly amazed at how little I can keep a secret. I almost gave away his birthday surprise party fifteen times. I don't know how to hold my feelings and thoughts back—but I haven't had to be devious. My life as a middle-class, cisgender, white lady is pretty damned stable. But on the college campus where I work, Tamar sits next to me and reminds me that each person I meet struggles with injustice. She asks me to withhold judgment when a student's actions smack of piracy or tricks. When peer advocates for students who've been sexually assaulted have their program put in limbo and they respond with angry protest and secret filming of administrators, it makes me very uncomfortable. Yet they are using what they have to reform an exploitative system.

Out in the world, human traffickers target foster kids because they won't be missed: those kids are in a liminal space between family and disaster. It only takes a moment to tip one way or the other. Lots of folks live in that liminal space and use what they have to get what they need, but we don't see them. Likewise, Judah didn't really see Tamar until she showed him his hypocrisy.

This is Tamar's lineage as well as being a Canaanite. She is somewhere between a virgin and a wife, somewhere between insider and outsider. She is on the edge of society, where tricksters are born and where God's power is most obvious. New things happen there that just can't happen in the staid, respectable middle. And in tricking those in power, Tamar is hilarious.

Put that in a knitting pattern.

Rahab and Bathsheba

Who's Naked Now?

> It happened, late one afternoon, when David rose from his couch and was walking about on the roof of the king's house, that he saw from the roof a woman bathing; the woman was very beautiful.
>
> —2 Samuel 11:2

Like Tamar's, Rahab's and Bathsheba's stories are not read at Sunday worship. If we know their stories at all, they are about illicit sex and a kind of tabloid shock. In Jesus' genealogy, Bathsheba isn't even referred to by name but as the wife of Uriah.

Like Tamar, Rahab and Bathsheba were foreigners and outsiders to the promise God gave to Abraham and Sarah. They were not supposed to know the God of Israel, and they were not supposed to amount to anything other than maybe a good lay. But Rahab's story is part of the convoluted and redemptive story of Joshua and all of Israel taking possession of the Promised Land. Her help is what opened the door for them. Bathsheba's story is part of the convoluted and redemptive story of King David, who was later confronted for his evil deeds and admitted to his sin; it was her child who died as punishment. With their own nakedness, these two women reveal the nakedness of the system they live in.

Rahab was a prostitute in the walled city of Jericho. Remember Jericho? The one where the walls just fell down in front of the Israelites? Rahab, the ancient rabbis said, was one of the top four most beautiful women in the world; even saying her name made you lust after her. So don't read this book out loud. In addition to making a living by getting naked, Rahab might also have been an innkeeper. Some say calling her a prostitute was a later addition to the story—that she was a legitimate businesswoman who didn't fit into the writers' categories for what women should be. But as in the case of Mary Magdalene, if she were a prostitute, that would mean there was more depth to Rahab's conversion. For someone in such a depraved profession to recognize the holiness of the God of Abraham, Isaac, and Jacob would be miraculous. Further, her conversion gives the rest of us some hope that we in our own depravity can participate in the love of God. Either way, however, the story isn't concerned with the morality of her profession. Either way, her home would have been a place of many comings and goings, a place to find information on all sorts of people.

One evening, just before the city gates were to be shut and all the people settled down for the night, there was a knock on Rahab's door. "Customers," she thought, not sure if she was pleased at the prospect of income or resigned to entertaining men for the night. She looked around the crowded common room out of habit, then stood and smoothed the robe over her breasts, taking care to let it gap open enticingly. Opening the door, she saw two men who looked . . . scared. Intrigued, she said, "Come in, come in," closing the door after them and preparing to relieve them of their nerves and their money. Looking at them in the light of the lamp, she realized they were looking around not out of sexual anxiety but in genuine fear. "Gentlemen, what's wrong?" she asked.

They looked at her, taking in her overwhelming beauty, then at each other. Then one took a deep breath and poured out their story about wandering in the desert for forty years, following their

God to the Promised Land, and how they were finally here—or, anyway, just over that rise—and God said to take over this land but first to scout it out and see who was here and what their fortifications were, and oh my gosh, the Promised Land is so green but also so different from what they'd thought, and could they just sleep here tonight?

Rahab looked them in the eyes and made her decision then and there. "Gentlemen, you may sleep here. And what's more, you're welcome to the hospitality of my house. You do know what we do here, right? Yes? Wonderful. I'll make up some beds, and we can take our pleasure." (Did they really partake of Rahab's body or not? The author of the book of Joshua is coyly silent.)

But in the midst of this conversation, there was another knock on the door. Knowing something was amiss, Rahab sent the two visitors up to the roof to hide under the flax that was drying there. Smoothing her robe over her breasts and taking a fortifying breath, Rahab opened the door to messengers from the king. "Spies have come from the enemy Israelites; they were seen in this neighborhood. The king demands you hand them over, whore." She said to the messenger, "Sure, there were a couple of guys here, but you know me: Why would I ask where they're from if they've got coin? We had sex, and then they left. If you ride fast, you might catch them." And she gestured vaguely toward the city gates. The search party believed her story, for what more could a prostitute hide? All her sins are revealed in the parting of her robe. They rode fast out of the city, the gate closing behind them.

She went up to the roof and sat down in front of the two men, her feet curled under her. "Listen," she said, "I know who you are. I know about the Red Sea and about how you killed all the Amorites." She swallowed and continued, "I know who your God is. I know your God is really God. I know my people are shitting themselves, they're so scared of you. I will not be afraid. I will help you if you will help my family—my parents, my siblings, all their children and dear ones. You will help my family, yes?"

The men looked at Rahab and saw not only a beautiful woman whose body they could reveal and take but also the truth of her words. They saw a woman at the head of her household, ready to do whatever it took to protect them. They saw a woman who had already done whatever it took. "Yes," they said, "if you tell no one about us, we will protect you and yours." They drew up a kind of verbal legal agreement: Rahab would hang a crimson cord from her window to show them where she was, her family would stay in the house, Rahab would keep their secret, and in return, the Israelites would spare her and her family the massacre of Jericho.

Rahab sent the spies on their way by lowering them through her window and down the outside of the wall of the city. And indeed, they kept their word. After the Israelites marched menacingly around Jericho and blew their trumpets every day for a week, after the walls suddenly crumbled to dust, after Rahab's neighbors ran in terror to get away from the oncoming army, Rahab and her family huddled together in her house, clinging to each other as they heard their neighbors begging for mercy. There came a knock at the door. Rahab stood and smoothed the robe over her breasts, taking care to let it gap open enticingly. Opening the door, she looked at the two men, this time she herself scared of what she might see. Without a word, they shepherded her and her family out of the ruined city and into their camp. The family received food and water and a tent of their own, a place of honor. Some say Rahab then married Joshua himself, and her grandchildren included prophets whose minds were as luminous as her own beauty: Jeremiah, Hilkiah, and even Hulda, who many years later found the lost scrolls of the Torah and instigated a spiritual renaissance in Israel.

Rahab the innkeeper, prostitute, and betrayer of her people was then held up as a heroic convert. Saint Paul and Saint James proved their theological points by using her as a magnificent example of good works or else as a phenomenal example of deep faith. "Clearly we are saved by our faith alone, just as Rahab believed in God!" "Obviously, we are saved by our good works, just as Rahab labored to save the spies!" Either way, her life was not easily defined. She was not just a prostitute. She was not just a hero. She was not just a body for invaders to take. She knew her *nephesh*, the Hebrew word for her self, her inner life, her thoughts and feelings. Like my seven-year-old daughter, who when we talked about a hymn in church that said we are God's, said with certainty, "No, Mama, I am my own," Rahab was herself before she was anyone else's.

Rahab's great-granddaughter-in-law Bathsheba was even less easy to define. Bathsheba was war spoils for a spoiled King David. She was a wife and mother and political manipulator. Bathsheba was married to an officer in King David's army named Uriah the Hittite, another foreigner. The Hittites were friendly with the Israelites, but still outsiders. It was the season for war, when kings went after what they wanted and fought hard for conquest. Most kings, anyway. King David was home in his comfy palace. Uriah was the one out fighting the war. And Bathsheba was at home, minding her own business.

She had just finished menstruating, so she was bathing herself to feel clean again and for spiritual purity. She filled a bowl with cool water and brought a towel from the pile of clean clothes. She opened her robe and laid it on the table nearby. Taking a cup and a small cloth, she poured the water over her hot skin, through her hair, over her throat, down her thighs. It felt good to be clean again; it was a kind of small new beginning, when the possibilities of her life were again available. What would she do today? How would she use this time outside the red tent? She dried herself off slowly, enjoying the feel of the towel and the light breeze that came through the window. Wait, the window? Wasn't she on the roof? Leonard Cohen said so, so it must be true. The stories we've told after the fact say she went onto her roof to bathe, possibly on purpose, hoping for her nakedness to be seen, or possibly because that's just what people did at the time. But that's not what the biblical story says. It says David was on the roof of his palace and saw her bathing. How did he do that? Perhaps he caught sight of her accidentally; perhaps he knew that vantage point afforded him views of many women's baths, wherever the women were taking them. Either way, when he saw her naked body, he *looked*.

Was he bored? Horny? Drunk on power? David, the greatest king of Israel, to whom God gave victory wherever he went, did what was right in his own eyes. He had her brought to him and slept with her. Bathsheba's feelings about this are cloaked in darkness: Was it consensual? Was she hoping for his favors? Did she take the opportunity presented? Did he take from her, and to redeem her worth, she consented to marriage? She never says a word in this story. The text doesn't condemn her for her actions with David, nor is the language about seduction, so we don't know.

When she missed her period the next month, Bathsheba sent a message to David telling him so. "Look what has happened. Are you going to step up?" King David did what any normal person would do: he recalled her husband Uriah from the war, tried to get him to go home and sleep with his wife so the baby would seem to be entirely legal, and when the officer refused, had him sent to the front lines to be killed. David even had Uriah carry the very orders that took his life to his superior officer himself. Long live the king, I guess. With Uriah out of the picture, David was free to marry Bathsheba and reveal her nakedness anytime he wanted.

Later on, the prophet Nathan confronted David, stripping away the layers of metaphorical clothing David had protected himself with, leaving him exposed. "You are the man who took the sheep from her shepherd and destroyed everything!" Bathsheba's presence revealed David's weakness. Her nakedness exposed his.

There's more to her story than being the seemingly passive participant in a sex scandal. The baby Bathsheba was carrying died soon after birth as punishment for David. When she later gave birth to Solomon (yes, that Solomon), she made sure he would be the next king, making her queen mother, chief wife, and kingmaker. In case you thought the weird sexual machinations were over, Solomon's rival for the throne later asked her to help him get her dead husband's concubine as a lover. Because why not? Women's bodies were pawns in a larger cultural game, but those pawns had plans of their own as well.

Rahab and Bathsheba's stories are part of larger, epic narratives about claiming the land promised by God. There's some question about whether the Israelites really did claim the land through bloody conquest or whether these are public relations spin to justify their already having lived there for generations. Either way, Rahab and Bathsheba's bodies and the bodies of thousands of their sisters are part of the Israelite claim to Canaan. So many Rahabs were killed in the massacre at Jericho and are killed every day by johns or pimps or brothers or fathers. So many Bathshebas were taken as wives because they could be. So many Bathshebas are taken as wives because they're not seen as people and Boko Haram or whomever thinks they deserve them.

When I was in junior high school, I walked home every day. Like many women, I got catcalled from the buses. Once another kid grabbed my ass as he passed me on the sidewalk. Somehow he thought I was available for the taking. As recently as last week, I was weeding the front garden of my campus ministry, and a guy in a van whistled and yelled, "I'd hit that!" Not that it matters, but I was wearing my clerical collar—ooh, sexy. When I jerked up, sneered at him, and flipped him off—pastors aren't immune to anger, you know—he winked and leered at me and drove away. While it's not nearly as violent as things that happen to women all over the world, it's also not merely awkward but part of a pattern. Our bodies are seen as public property. Somehow we are not expected to have our own desires and thoughts. Somehow it's a surprise that we might be more than prostitutes or wife material.

A few years ago, the LGBTQ group at the university I work for did a program called "Born This Way," inspired, of course, by modern-day theologian Lady Gaga. They invited the people who came to stand up, introduce ourselves, and say something about a part of our body we don't like much. We talked some about body image and about what our bodies are "supposed" to be like. Then the leaders each spoke about something they loved about their bodies. And then stripped down to their underpants. They looked so vulnerable and uncertain. It was shocking and beautiful. They invited us to do the same, if we liked. Most folks didn't strip down, but we all shared, a bit tearfully.

The stories of Rahab and Bathsheba are likely more legend than history, but as with all good stories, that's not the point. What matters is what we do with them. It's not just those terrible men doing this violence, obviously. Women have participated in shaming and hurting each other as well. Rahab and Bathsheba are part of an epic narrative about how to be human to each other. How do we care rather than take? How do we offer rather than manipulate? How do we trust rather than destroy?

We think of nakedness, no matter the gender, as weakness, and maybe it is. There's no protection, nothing to hide behind. Our soft bits outside and inside our bodies can be hurt or mocked. Rahab made her living taking off her clothes, but she was even more naked when she sat on the roof and revealed her vulnerability to the Israelite spies. She laid herself bare in the hope they would not take advantage. Bathsheba was just naked, caring for her body's needs, when she was made vulnerable by David's lust. She was laid bare and became a tool in someone else's story. For Rahab and Bathsheba, the weakness of nakedness became strength. Their weakness disarmed the powerful.

Ruth

Who Are You Responsible For?

When Boaz had eaten and drunk, and he was in a contented mood, he went to lie down at the end of the heap of grain. Then she came quietly and uncovered his feet, and lay down. At midnight the man was startled and turned over, and there, lying at his feet, was a woman! He said, "Who are you?" And she answered, "I am Ruth, your servant; spread your cloak over your servant, for you are next-of-kin."

—RUTH 3:7–9

There's this story we tell about Ruth; I hear it at weddings sometimes, or at Thanksgiving. Jews tell it at Shavuot, the Festival of the Harvest. Ruth is this pretty, clean, hardworking woman who catches the eye of a wealthy landowner, and their union means both a plentiful harvest (because: pagan fertility rites) and that Israel will be politically relevant again (because: fertility rites aren't just for pagans anymore). It's sheaves of wheat and euphemisms about sex done up in a kind of sepia-toned romance novel.

But of course, the Bible is rarely straightforward, and Ruth's story is not unambiguous. Turns out, it's also about the threat of sexual violence, about what a woman is worth, and about how we take care of each other. It's also about foreigners—the worst kind of illegal aliens—taking our food and our husbands and becoming a new nation when the old one was just fine, thank you very much. God has an embarrassing habit of breaking the rules, particularly the one that says, "No outsiders allowed."

Ruth's story begins with her mother-in-law, Naomi, and a famine in Judah. Naomi's family—her husband, Elimilech, and her two sons—travel to a neighboring country to escape. No, that's not right; that doesn't really communicate. Naomi's family are refugees from a natural disaster. They hung on as long as they could, because after all, this was their land, and Elimilech's father's land, and his father's before him. This was the land they had tilled and planted and made a green space to raise their boys. Their strong boys, whom Naomi remembers nursing in that chair like it was this morning. Their beautiful boys, whose fat thighs Naomi kissed and sighed over. Their grown boys, for whom Naomi now gives up her dinner so they can eat. This was their land and their life, but now it is a place of death. So they turn their backs on the land where they've buried their hearts, and they search for food and security in Moab of all places.

You can't hear the disdain just in reading the text. Read it slowly like it's something slimy you found on your shoe: Moab. You have no idea, do you? The Moabites, friends, they're filthy. Their whole tribe began when Lot and his daughters survived the catastrophe at Sodom. The daughters thought they were the only people left alive, so they got their dad drunk and . . . yeah, they slept with him and got pregnant. That's where Moab came from. Oh, and you know that story about Ehud the judge and how he stabbed that one king who was so fat Ehud's sword *and his whole arm* got stuck inside him, and then the guards were too embarrassed to go in to see what was going on because the whole thing happened while the king was on the potty? Yeah, that king was from Moab. They're filthy and ridiculous.

So Naomi and her husband and her sons arrive exhausted in Moab with some of their most precious and useful things from home—her best pots and pans, the tent, blankets to protect from the night's chill, dresses, books, a delicate vase given as a gift, and that chair Elimilech made, where she sat with her babies. They settle down, because as filthy and ridiculous as the Moabites are supposed to be, they have food, and it feels like the family hasn't really eaten in a year. Naomi and Elimilech find a small tract of land and plant some seeds and raise a couple of sheep. It turns out that the Moabites aren't as bad as everyone said, and the boys fall in love. So now Naomi's family adds two more: Ruth and Orpah. Things are going well. Until they aren't. Because a sickness strikes the area, and Naomi's husband dies. And then, then her sons die, one after the other. Can you even imagine?

They move again. *Again.* Fewer people this time. Fewer things to carry, but what is left is so much more precious—the chair, of course, and a couple of pots. And so much is left behind again. Empty homes with the potential for children, rooms filled with memories, neighbors who cleaned after we were sick, neighbors who planted and harvested and milked with us. Neighbors who fell ill when our husbands did. Neighbors who died.

As they leave, Naomi turns to her daughters-in-law and says, "Go back." She says, "The future in Judah is uncertain [read, 'probably shitty'] for foreigners like you. Your families will take care of you. Go with them."

Both Ruth and Orpah say, "No, we will go with you, our mother, the mother of our husbands. We are family; that means a thing. Don't send us away."

Naomi shoos them away like they're Old Yeller, telling them she's too old to birth more husbands for them and what does she have to offer them? Indeed, she thinks, what *does* she have to offer? The sweetness of youth has turned to bitterness with experience. Her only value was in her sons. The world in which she lives called her a good wife and mother for bearing them and nursing them and training them up to be good men, and now they are dead. Her little boys, who were the light in her darkness and who still brought her pretty things they'd found in their travels, are dead, so what can she possibly have left?

Orpah and Ruth weep at Naomi's despair, because they see their own lives in hers. They weep for the children they have not had, maybe even for the children they bore but who did not survive. Orpah squares her shoulders and shakes out her skirts, as though leaving something behind again, and she turns back to walk the leagues to her family's pastures, with the thin hope on her face that family members will be there and will care for her.

Naomi holds Ruth by the shoulders, both faces wet and contorted with grief. Naomi says, "You must go. You must go. Orpah has already left, and there is nothing for you in Judah. There is nothing for you in me. I am bitter and empty. Just . . . just go."

Ruth presses her lips together, squeezes her eyelids together to stop the flow of tears. Her eyes open and she says,

"Where you go, I will go;
    where you lodge, I will lodge;
your people shall be my people,
    and your God my God.
Where you die, I will die—
    there will I be buried."

And they turn to face the long walk around the Dead Sea toward Bethlehem.

It turns out that Naomi has a distant cousin, Cousin Boaz, in Bethlehem who has been doing well for himself. Ruth, knowing she and Naomi have arrived in Israel with little more than the clothes they are wearing, prepares herself to glean. Now, gleaning isn't as bad as begging in the market square, but it's pretty bad. Only the most desperate go to grain fields to collect wheat that falls on the ground or is left on the stalks at the edges of the field. Ruth has never even considered it, even in the darkest days of her husband's illness. Yet they have nothing, so early the first morning, she breathes in and out, prays to Naomi's God, Yahweh, and goes.

She plucks grains for hours under the hot sun. She pulls whole heads from plants here and there but spends much of the time crouched down to pick up grains scattered by the main harvesters. Each precious grain of wheat drops into the basket she makes by pulling up her skirts. Certainly Ruth is used to hard work, being a farmer's wife, but this is so much more. When does the exhaustion set in? When does her back begin to ache and her throat balk at swallowing because she has no water jar? Was there a time before gleaning?

Hours into her labors, the man himself, Cousin Boaz, comes to oversee his employees. As the story goes, he sees her from afar, the sweat of her brow making her face glow and her beauty shine (see "sepia-toned romance novel"). He asks after her and is told she is Ruth the Moabite (read, "Ruth the Dirty Foreigner"). He says to her, "I've heard about you, how you care for your mother-in-law, how you risked everything to come here though you have no one to rely on." It would be enough for him only to know her story and not look down on her, but then he says, "Harvest grain not just along the edges but in the heart of the field; take even the grain my workers have already harvested. And for goodness sakes, drink some of the water they have; you need to hydrate." This, we are to assume, is a kind of flirting.

When Ruth arrives home in the evening with piles and piles of grain as well as, the Bible tells us, leftovers from the dinner Boaz insisted on offering her, Naomi's eyes light up. She looks at Ruth, and the possibility of marriage and children wells up in her eyes. Ruth has brought food, yes, but has she brought more than food? Could she bear sons to replace the ones Naomi has lost? They couldn't possibly replace . . . but maybe they could.

Months pass, glossed over in the text with a phrase about Ruth's hard work in the field and her implied chastity because of it. Then one night, Naomi comes to Ruth with her best dress folded carefully over her arm. She has a necklace her husband gave her when they were young and uninhibited; she had kept it through their migrations as a reminder that she had once been desirable, full of her husband's body and love. She has as well a small jar of nard, the spicy and expensive oil whose scent fills the room when opened. Ruth looks at these things, and a smile of recognition grows on her face. Naomi says, "Boaz is working on the threshing floor tonight. Alone. Go to him." She holds out the dress, the necklace, and the nard. Ruth's eyes sparkle with possibility as she takes them, dresses in them, begins to feel skin prickle with arousal. She opens the nard and pours some on her wrists, between her breasts, on her lower back. The smell is intoxicating. She closes her eyes and feels her body sway as she breathes in and out. And she goes out to the threshing floor, the place where, prosaically, the useful grains of wheat are removed from the hard chaff, and where, poetically, lovers come together, babies are made, and the harvest becomes a symbol for erotic refilling of the people.

There on the threshing floor, Boaz has fallen asleep after a long day. Ruth sees him stretched out like a feast for her. She lies next to him and uncovers his feet—a charming euphemism for his penis. He wakes up (with a start? in growing pleasure?) and sees Ruth the Dirty Foreigner, now dirty in another way. His nostrils fill with the scent of nard and of fresh grain; his body warms to her. And she doesn't simply let him have his way with her, as Naomi suggested, but tells him how it will be. She says, "Cover me with your cloak," which means "Protect me and marry me and be intimate with me. Bring me close to your body and to your heart." It's a bit romantic, but it's also heavily sexual and not a little bit demanding. The text makes a nice Hollywood fade-out, like the one in *Breakfast at Tiffany's*, where you just *know* they had sex.

And everything changes. Ruth is no longer foreigner but family. Like the grain harvest, she has a new beginning, a new creation, a new connection. Not even Boaz's awkward speech before they make love about how he will deal with the bureaucracy of claiming her as his wife can ruin the moment. Pillow talk is hard, guys.

The next morning, Boaz fills her skirts with grain again (grain or "grain"? Know what I'm saying?) and sends her back home with the promise that he will come for her. The story suddenly shifts away from Ruth and Naomi onto the men and the exciting world of real estate and inheritance. They sit at the city gate, upright men doing upright things according to the laws they have written. Boaz declares to the only other distant cousin present, "Naomi's land is available for claiming. Do you want it?" The man says, "Yes, of course." Boaz says, "Wonderful, just one small thing; I'm sure it won't be a bother. You're also claiming Ruth the Dirty Foreigner as your wife, and the land will go to her kids when you die. That's cool, right?" The man says, "Now that you mention it, I don't really have the resources to farm more land." He then takes off his sandal and hands it to Boaz, which we all know is the universal sign of giving away your right to claim something. Boaz smiles predatorily and says, "I couldn't possibly. Well, if you insist."

Here all the people congratulate Boaz on his upcoming nuptials and say, "We always knew Ruth the Dirty Foreigner was good people! May she give you many sons! May she be like Tamar, who dressed up like a whore to trick her father-in-law into impregnating her and bringing her back into the fold!" Congratulations have changed over the years, I guess. Even though Ruth has been brought into the family, she is still a bit of an outsider. And her baby, the text tells us, becomes Naomi's baby, filling Naomi's emptiness. Ruth doesn't live an idyllic life but an ambiguous one. She's the great-grandmother of David the greatest king of Israel, and she is a sexually threatening foreigner. She is a good wife and mother and also breadwinner and trickster.

Ruth's story isn't one about war or politics but about private lives and a personal God. Ruth is living the quotidian mysteries, the struggle and divine beauty in everyday life. I imagine Ruth and Naomi knew about Moses speaking to God through a bush-that-was-burning-but-not-consumed and Ezekiel's visions of a God-mobile bizarre enough to make anyone's head reel. Their lives were filled with the presence of God in much less dramatic ways. Let's be real. Most of us don't have burning-bush moments or cosmic visions; we deal with grumpy coworkers and children's toys on the floor and paying bills and good-bye kisses as we leave for work or school or whatever. God who is THE I AM is also God who simply is. In the midst of scripture about the future of nations and leaders, here is a story about food and sex and bureaucracy.

There is bad news here (or maybe just news, a clear-eyed description of our lives): things are sometimes really hard, really damn hard. There is also good news here: a baby in the midst of misery and childlessness. They go hand in hand, the good news and the bad, like Ruth and Naomi walking around the Dead Sea toward Bethlehem.

Mary Theotokos

More than Meets the Eye

> When the angels had left them and gone into heaven, the shepherds said to one another, "Let us go now to Bethlehem and see this thing that has taken place, which the Lord has made known to us." So they went with haste and found Mary and Joseph, and the child lying in the manger. When they saw this, they made known what had been told them about this child; and all who heard it were amazed at what the shepherds told them. But Mary treasured all these words and pondered them in her heart.
>
> —LUKE 2:15–19

We don't know much about Mary the mother of Jesus. There are those famous stories about riding the donkey to Bethlehem and nudging Jesus into making wine out of water for a friend's wedding. There's the story about the angel telling her she'd be having God's kid and then her long, folk-protest song we call the Magnificat—kind of a first-century version of "We Shall Overcome." She was at the crucifixion and in the upper room when the disciples chose who would replace Judas after his messy suicide. But even so, she's mysterious. What was it like to have those shepherds crowd into the intimate and exhausted space after giving birth? What was it like to raise the Son of God, who may or may not have raised sparrows from the dead when he was in elementary school? What was it like to watch him die and rise and ascend? What was it like to outlive her firstborn?

We think of her as a mother first, don't we? She held in her womb not only a baby but God; early Christians called her The-otokos, "god-bearer." We call her the greatest mother who ever lived and also an unwed teen mom. We say she was perpetually a virgin and that she had several more kids after Jesus. Mary meek and mild. Mary accepting of what comes. We certainly don't think of her like fiery Ezekiel or lamenting Jeremiah. They had a word to speak to the people, and Mary is just, well, she's just a mom, isn't she? We moms do a lot of things and have a lot of responsibilities, but in the end, it's all about hearth and home. That's what they'd have you believe. I don't know who "they" are, but they're pretty convincing, aren't they? Somewhere in an unused storeroom in our brains, we know that's not right. It's not right that anyone is "just a mom," and it's not right that Mary was "just a mom" either. She's got something different going on, but it's something we've had a hard time putting our finger on.

From the beginning, Mary was something more than we expected. I suppose it depends on which beginning you look at. The before-she-was-a-glimmer-in-her-parents'-eyes beginning or the first-appearance-with-the-angel-and-divine-impregnation beginning. The first one is a fascinating and convoluted argument called the Immaculate Conception. Essentially, the problem was this: (1) Original sin, the church says, is passed down from generation to generation through sex. Because we're born, we're sinful. Thanks, mom and dad! (2) Jesus, having been born, must then have been sinful. The horror! No, that simply can't be. Jesus was sinless, because obviously. But how? Like so: (3) For centuries, scientists thought babies were made solely out of the dad's semen and implanted in the mom's belly. Mom's just an incubator; therefore, she's not contributing to the genetic material of original sin. In a brand-new scientific discovery (1677 maybe), it turned out that's entirely incorrect. (4) So if Jesus was made from God and Mary, we've got to do something about Mary's contribution to the potential for Jesus to sin. (5) Therefore, in 1854, the Catholic Church, bless them, declared that Mary herself was without original sin so that Jesus would also be without original sin. Science!

The second beginning is more poetic. It's the Annunciation, Mary's origin story. She was not some random woman whom God, all Zeus-like, impregnated with a dove or a shower of gold. She was chosen, maybe because she didn't run away, because she pushed back, trying to understand. She settled into the moment and consented to being the caretaker of the baby God. This is important because, no matter what arguments we make about God's omnipotence and predestination, God wants us to choose. One of my students says, "God is all about enthusiastic consent." In twenty-first-century America, where Brock Turner served only half of a laughably short sentence for raping an unconscious woman and doesn't seem to show any remorse, questions of consent are not idle. God, in the guise of the angel, said, "Mary, do you want this baby?" and she said, "Yes. Yes, I do."

What's interesting is that while Mary's first story is obviously a birth announcement, it much more closely fits a different form of biblical writing, the prophetic call. The form goes like this: encounter an angel; angel calls you to do something difficult; object to the call; you are reassured and given a sign. This is precisely what happens when Gabriel drops by Mary's house. Like Moses, Gideon, Isaiah, Jeremiah, and Ezekiel before her, Mary is called to prophetic action.

In this beginning, while visiting her cousin Elizabeth, she sang long and loud about gratitude and her own unworthiness to be a mother and how overwhelmingly giddy it had made her. She sang about God's attentiveness to the people with no power and about God's power to remake the world. She sang about justice and regime change and transformation. "This child will change everything," she sang. "This child has already changed everything." In the end, a breathless silence, and then cousin Elizabeth applauded and called her "Prophetess," and they laughed.

From there, the text skips over the actual pregnancy. It's not important to the story the writers are telling, but it's so important to those of us who've been pregnant. I remember the early days of my pregnancies—the painful joints, the exhaustion, and the fluttering in my belly, which I thought was the baby but was only gas. And later there was the fluttering that took my breath away while I was driving, and I cried and grabbed for Leighton's hand to feel the tiny elbow pressing up against my belly. When my Jackson stretched and pushed a bony part outward, I pushed it back, tapping it like a message, and his elbow tapped me back. Mary must have felt all the same things—the discomfort of building a person and the growing awe and connection with that little person.

When Matthew tells the birth story, there's no fanfare. Joseph kindly didn't break their engagement when he found out she was pregnant. They married, she had the baby, and they lived in a house, where the magi visited them with fancy, impractical gifts. Done.

When Luke tells it, Joseph and a very pregnant Mary traveled by donkey almost seventy miles to Bethlehem so they could be counted. Or taxed. Something bureaucratic, anyway. They found shelter only in the last place they looked, kind of like in a fairy tale. You almost expect there to be a witch there giving them shelter in exchange for enchanted shoes. In the barn were the oxen standing around and the fluffy sheep, and it was all warm and charming—or gross and smelly, depending on your experience of barns. Meanwhile, an army of angels appeared to some random shepherds nearby and sang to them and told them to go to this one barn where the savior of the world had been born. It's all very epic.

Every mom has a birth story, and they all feel epic. I actually fell asleep while in labor with my daughter. I'd been up for thirty hours by the time it was really happening, and between every push, I fell asleep. I'm not even kidding. Mary's birth story is the one we tell over and over, but the part we don't tell, because Matthew and Luke don't tell us, is her looking at her new baby. Mary swaddled her baby boy in that warm, dirty stable, the tight cloth comforting the baby Jesus so he mercifully stopped crying. She stared down at his round cheeks, trying to memorize the softness of his skin, the shape of his ears. Maybe—probably—she wept with joy and terror at this new thing. "Why didn't anyone say? How could I love someone this much? We're connected forever, little one."

Afterward, Matthew says, the family fled to Egypt to avoid King Herod's jealous wrath. Luke says they took him to the temple to be blessed. Matthew and Luke had different ideas about what makes a good story, I guess. What's not in the stories is Mary's raising Jesus to be a good man and a good Jew. His childhood just isn't in there. Lots of people have speculated about what happened in that time period. Did he raise a sparrow back to life, as the later "Infancy Gospel of James" said? Did he travel to China and invent kung fu, as Christopher Moore wrote? Surely he backtalked Mary and stayed out late as a teenager? Dunno.

The closest we get is when the family went to Jerusalem for the Passover festival—days-long celebrations and prayer services and reconnecting with old friends, all in service of remembering that we were slaves, we wandered, and we came home. The family went, celebrated, prayed, reconnected, and then left. They were part of a big caravan of folks from their town, so when Mary and Joseph couldn't find tween Jesus, they weren't worried—until a couple of days into their return journey. Then they worried. They went back, looking everywhere for him, looking at animal carcasses along the road with increasing panic. By the time they got back to Jerusalem, Mary was beside herself. What could have happened to her little boy? Eventually, they found him in the temple, calmly explaining finer points of theology to men four times his age. Mary said, "Young man, you come here right now. You are in big trouble." Jesus turned to her and said, "Ma, didn't you know I'd be in my father's house?" and went back to teaching. He was twelve, he was growing up, and he was already pushing away from home into the cruel, intriguing world.

Years later, Mary took him to the wedding of some friends in nearby Cana. Midway through the party, the wine ran out. When I tell this story to my daughter, she asks me why this was a problem. I mean, they could have drunk water or milk or juice. Wine was the safe bet at the time, both for not having germs in it and for revelry. So Mary said, "Jesus, you should do something about the wine. You know, that thing you do at our house all the time?" And Jesus said, "Not now, Ma, I'm busy." Mary tutted and turned to the sommelier and said, "Just do whatever he says. It'll be worth it." I imagine Jesus sighing affectionately and then making the best wine and then the best party ever. Mary wasn't just his mom. She saw him for the man he was becoming.

That made it so painful just a few years later, when her son was at the height of his ministry. He was healing all kinds of people and preaching three and four gigs a day. In one of those places, he sat with his disciples arrayed around him, looking at him adoringly, and Mary approached with a couple of his siblings. (I previously mentioned he wasn't an only child. Perpetual virgin, my ass.) Someone said, "Hey, yo, Jesus, your ma's here." And Jesus—who Mary remembered crying on her shoulder when he skinned his knees and once refusing to eat hummus for a week—said, "Who is my mother? Who are my siblings? You here are my mother and siblings, you who follow God."

She saw how special he was, beyond being her baby boy, and here he was setting her aside. Obviously, Jesus and Matthew and Luke are making a larger point here, but for us reading it—mothers or fathers—we know that to have your own son say that is painful. Maybe Mary thought, "You are my son; I *made* you. And you say I'm not your mother to make a rhetorical point? It's not that I'm angry, though I really am. I'm hurt." I suppose this is an indissoluble part of parenthood—our children's rejection. Not necessarily intentional, but real.

And then came the place she feared the most. Maybe she didn't see it coming exactly, but on some level, Mary knew her son's path would not end with fat grandchildren. To think on the death of your child is one of the worst things—and one of the most common things for parents. The ferocity of my love for my daughter and son scares me sometimes. What I would do to protect them from harm. How hollow my belly would be without them. And how proud of them I am, how much I trust them to take on the world. It fills my chest fit to burst sometimes.

That Friday morning, Mary had been so tired. Nothing was as it should be. Her little boy, her round-faced little boy, was in prison. She'd trusted that he knew what he was doing, and even still, how could she not be overwhelmed by fear? Every moment had been pregnant with unshed tears. And then, then he left. He passed. He died. He was just . . . gone.

Mary isn't in any of the resurrection appearances, and I totally get it. To have your worst fears realized in such a brutal fashion is unimaginable. She left. She wandered the streets, maybe, or left the town entirely and sat in the darkness outside the walls. She went home and made hummus—the kind he eventually liked—and fed her family and slept and got up and did it again.

I can't imagine Jesus didn't make a resurrection appearance to his mother at some point. Collapsing into each other, tears and snot flowing, then maybe a hard slap on his cheek to remind him who she was. Surely, surely, he went to see her after the tomb and showing Thomas his wounds and making brunch for the disciples on the beach. Maybe that's why she showed up again in the upper room after Jesus was taken bodily into heaven, but it's just a mention. She was there, one of the "certain women" present to figure out what to do next. People were still sick and greedy and asleep. Mary pondered, "What have you done, my boy? I can't tell yet."

What will you do, my children? I wonder, Abby and Jackson, will you be kind and courageous, or will you be bullies? Will your sins be glaringly obvious or subtle? Will you speak for the voiceless and help them find their voices? Will you find someone who will love you the way I do, only not the way I do? Will you love them? Will your lives leave the world better than you found it? Will mine? I don't know. But I hope so.

My Enneagram teacher says hope is a terrible concept, that it teaches dependence on a false future rather than on the depth and realness of now. If indeed hope is the pap offered by politicians and smiley megachurch pastors to get us to give them money, I agree. But I don't think that's what Mary is about. She considers wondering to be a kind of hope, and asking questions about reality and God's action to be a form of justice. She sees the reality of community and social change and her son's short life and in them possibility. It is the gift of her contemplative, pondering heart. Even when things seem bleakest, light shines in the darkness, and the darkness cannot overcome it.

From that light comes her prophetic song: the Magnificat. I'm not sure why we've lost the image of a prophetic Mary. We are left with a quiet, obedient mother without the firebrand language of the Magnificat, but that song is just as much a part of her as beatifically giving birth in a stable. Mary is more complex than we remember, more challenging than we expect. I'll be honest here: When we read the Magnificat in church, I'm startled each time by how difficult it is. She speaks the good news that the lowly will be lifted up, the lofty will be brought low, and the rich sent away empty, which sometimes doesn't sound like good news to me. It sounds like a threat.

If the rich are to be sent away empty and I am the rich (it's all relative, but compared with much of the world, most of us in America are), then something's going to change. It's easier to put God and people like Mary into calmer, more quietly loving boxes, so we don't have to deal with the change they call for. But Mary breaks out of that box and tells us lovingly but firmly, "No, darlin'. This is not how we do things." She is a prophet, bearing God's difficult but good Word to the world.

And she is a contemplative. After her son's birth, Luke tells us Mary "treasured all these words and pondered them in her heart." She looks at her son and the world and sees them clearly. She sees the patterns of human behavior and how we consistently screw things up. She sees what can be: the potential for beauty and compassion and grace.

We need Mary's clear sight, because mothers lose their children all the time—to death, sure, and to drugs and sundry other bad things, and to adulthood. To bear up under that, we have to become contemplatives. Of course, we can just drown in our emotions or pretend they don't exist, but that way lies madness and a culture of surface things. We need to be Mary, not because she was meek and mild, but because she was a prophet and a contemplative, and those things make us better mothers.

2

Hebrew Women

I'm a bit odd as a preacher because I almost always choose to preach on the assigned Hebrew scripture as opposed to the Gospel. (By the way, "Old Testament" is so last year—also slightly offensive, as it implies that these books are themselves so last year. One testament is not better than the other, so we now try for different names for them, like Hebrew and Christian scriptures.)

It's not that I don't like Jesus. He's pretty great; I'm a fan. But I've always struggled more with stories from the Hebrew scriptures. They've got a lot of complexity that doesn't get talked about so much. We paint them with a single brush, "that scary Old Testament God," and call it a day, but there's a lot of grace mixed in with the judgment. So the Gospel for a given Sunday might be "the feeding of the five thousand" or something equally meaty, but I'm going to dive deep into Ezekiel or Judith or Proverbs because whatever that passage is, it probably frustrates me. I figure if I'm frustrated by it, so are other people. (You could make the case that I could be equally likely to preach on something from Paul, because that guy, man, I want to have words with him.)

I also have to admit that I want to spin those stories. I want them to be better, less awkward, less patriarchal. I want to control how people read them—make sure the context and the nuances are in there. But I'm not in control, not of this or even of my own journey. This last year of my life, when my father lost his sight and my brother went to rehab and a couple of my students decided to leave the ministry, and you know, the world continued to suck, I realized how not in control I am. Involved, yes. In control, no.

These women's stories are awkward; there's no getting around it. They're painful and difficult, and they can't be controlled. We're not that much different nowadays. Some things have changed, but we still fight each other over men, we still care for our elders, and we still follow our own inner authority for good or ill. It's awkward to be aware of how far we've come and how far we still have to go.

I have a high tolerance for awkward, though, so let's dive in.

Asherah

So God Had a Wife, Maybe? Probably.

> The Israelites did what was evil in the sight of the LORD, forgetting the LORD their God, and worshipping the Baals and the Asherahs.
>
> —JUDGES 3:7

She was erased.

Like math sums done wrong or a letter phrased poorly, bits of her were scraped away and wiped off the page, as carelessly as if she did not exist. And in a way, I suppose she doesn't anymore. Her presence has been denied for generations; her story has become one of absence. She was Asherah. She was Mother of the Gods, she was the Lion Lady, and she it was who subdued the sea. She was the wife of Yahweh. She was the embodiment of nourishment; her breasts fed multitudes. She represented not only survival but plenty. Her hips birthed gods; her presence created abundant harvests. The people made sacrifices to her—grain and animals, even their children from time to time. They wove tremendous tapestries for her; they walked through fire for her. They stood in awe of the universe and its beauty and power, and they saw her and Yahweh in control of it all. She was worshipped with him in every home in the countryside. Or she was for a time.

Long after those creation myths were first told—maybe in the 500s BCE, when the people of Israel were exiled in Babylon and were overwhelmed with sadness and confusion—the stories changed. The people struggled to understand why this calamity had fallen on them, why the temple, God's house, had been destroyed, and where God even was. The religious authority began to blame the people's worship of foreign gods, saying Asherah and Baal were lovers. Baal was violent and clearly the god of foreigners, not of good Israelites. Only there wasn't often such a clear line between foreigners and Israelites. It wasn't always so obvious who were "us" and who were "them" in early Palestine.

Do you remember that story about Elijah going up against Asherah's 400 prophets? The story they told about that was a travesty. Elijah mocked Asherah and Baal and challenged their prophets to call down fire to burn a carcass. The story says it didn't work and Elijah's prayer did—even after he'd soaked the carcass and the altar with gallons of water. Elijah had all of Baal's 450 prophets killed; all of them died screaming because the people in charge thought they were a threat to Yahweh and to order and decency. And what happened to Asherah's 400 prophets? Did they survive? No idea. She wasn't worth following up.

Then some of the learned folks in the city decided she was made up, that she wasn't real. "Yahweh is the only God," they said, and the good kings tore down her high places and the sacred poles and trees dedicated to her. They had nothing good to say about her and her followers in Deuteronomy, Judges, Kings, and Chronicles. Not a single good word. Gideon destroyed her high places at night, under a cloak of darkness. King Josiah, that righteous man, didn't just cut down the poles, he burned them. He didn't just destroy the altars, he crushed them into dust. And he dug up the graves of the people there on the high places and set their bones on the dust of her altar and burned them, too. Strong actions against someone who didn't exist.

In the histories of Israel, they wanted to have it both ways. They insisted Israel only ever had one God the people worshipped, the God of Abraham, Isaac, and Jacob (and Sarah, Rebecca, Rachel, and Leah). Period. But they also insisted all of their heroes root out the foreign gods and their worshippers. Which was it? Was she real to the people, or wasn't she? All those standing stones the righteous kings and judges cut down and all her high places they destroyed—what were they for? If she wasn't real, in the end, what were they for?

They got prudish. They rejected Asherah because she was sexy and strong and off-message. They tried to erase her because they thought she was the cause of their problems. When the kings did what was evil in the sight of Yahweh, it was to worship her, to rebuild her high places and plant sacred groves of trees. When the people were righteous in the sight of Yahweh, it was to destroy all of that. We don't remember now whether any of that actually happened. But the story we tell—it's of violence and fear and rejection.

Now, thousands of years after those holy books were written, scholars have rediscovered her and the bare-breasted clay totems buried for centuries. They speak her names and write of her totems, her sacred trees, her high places with their rough and beautiful altars, and they don't know which names to call her: Asherah, Astarte, Anat, Qudshu, Queen of Heaven. She wasn't better than Yahweh or Ba'al, but she was there, standing on the same ground. At creation, our book of Genesis says, Yahweh turned to her and her children the Elohim and asked for wisdom, since the earth creatures he'd made had disobeyed him. Folks said the people of the land rejected the true God Yahweh, that they took up worshipping foreign gods, false gods, Asherah. But she was there from the beginning. Wasn't she?

She's there between the lines of Hebrew, like the feeling you get when you try to push the positive ends of two magnets together. You can feel the energy pushing between them, even though the space looks empty. Between the lines of Hebrew, where her sacred poles were torn down and she isn't even named, there is energy pushing back. Maybe she didn't exist—maybe she was just a quality of Yahweh that developed a name like Wisdom or Glory—or maybe these are stories we tell only to clarify that Yahweh is the only one.

It's hard to remember so much now. Those who wrote, wrote what they knew, but it's been so long. They wrote of Yahweh and of theology and of war and of themselves—men—doing manly things. What did they know of woman? What could they have known? Some knew, since many men came to worship at her high places. They sacrificed to Yahweh and to her, but when they wrote, where was she?

Asherah is not the only one.

She is being erased.

She is Sylvia Ray Rivera and Marsha P. Johnson, the queens who began the Stonewall riots in June 1969. She and many others were there at the gay bar the night decades of oppression and extortion and shame came to a head. The cops came to raid the bar yet again, and they said no. They got violent—because what else could they do when they'd been mistreated for so long? It wasn't a temper tantrum from entitled, spoiled kids; it was survival after years of abuse. They were the ones to throw bricks and to resist arrest and to dance a kick line down Christopher Street toward the oncoming cops. They were the black and Latino queens whose white activist friends didn't show up to support their cause, though they'd marched with them so many times. When Hollywood made a movie about Stonewall, they were not there. In the movie, the riots were started by a safe, middle-American white boy. But they were there. They were fabulous.

They are being erased.

They are the Armenian population of Turkey, massacred in April 1915. The Ottoman Empire found them . . . objectionable. Armenians couldn't testify in court against the Muslim majority.

They couldn't ride on horses or camels. They were spat on. And then the government decided they were a security risk. The government thought they were worthless, except when they thought they were powerful enough to share state secrets with Russia. So they killed their men in droves. Soldiers forced the rest of them to march into the desert without food or water. They beat them and raped them. Most of them died before arriving anywhere. The newspapers around the world reported about it, were horrified by what the Ottomans had done: eight hundred thousand or maybe even a million and a half dead. The country refused to admit that anything was amiss. Even now, Turkey will not admit to the word *genocide*. To be sure, many speak of atrocities and even of the systematic nature of their extermination, calling it a shameful act. But it cannot be called genocide. The word wasn't coined until afterward, so what happened simply wasn't genocide. It's a technicality, I guess, that it was coined to refer to this exact event. At the 2015 annual remembrance day, President of the United States Barack Obama didn't even use the word. We can't risk pissing off our military allies for the sake of truth, can we?

She is being erased.

She was Henrietta Lacks, a black woman from Virginia whose fatal cancer saved thousands of lives. When she was diagnosed with cervical cancer in 1951, the doctors took a sample of the cancer without asking her. The act was common for the time, really. What difference did it make to a poor, black woman? She died, but her cancer cells didn't. If you're a researcher, this is stunning—shocking even. Normally, cancer cells die quickly outside their normal environment, so researchers spend at least as much time keeping them alive as they do actually researching. Hers didn't die. Her cells are called, with some awe, immortal. And thousands of researchers use them every day, calling them HeLa cells, not knowing that HeLa is short for Henrietta Lacks, not knowing that they came from her, that they *are* her. Her family didn't understand when they were asked about it years later. They were horrified that part of her still lived, that they'd not known or been asked about using her illness for others. She is erased, yet she saves lives.

They are being erased.

They are the slaves brought over from Africa, stolen from their homes, beaten, raped, deprived, made miserable and alone. They are the system of oppression and ownership of people that the state of Texas erased by writing in their schoolbooks, "The Atlantic Slave Trade . . . brought millions of workers from Africa to the southern United States to work on agricultural plantations." Workers, they called them. As though they were paid. As though they chose this work. As though those plantations weren't a kind of hell.

They are being erased.

They are the heretics of the Christian church.

They asked questions people didn't always want to hear. They wondered aloud about what made Communion work and whether priests' sins made it not work. They questioned why God seemed to be absent despite having promised to be with us till the end of the age. They wondered if we were born sinful or if we learned sin along with virtue. They thought they were doing right, and maybe they were. Maybe they were wrong; that's possible, too. But to burn the pages they labored and prayed over, to exile them to wilderness lands, to kill them even—how could we? They were our brothers and sisters. We can't erase them or their ideas without consequences. And one of the many consequences was failure to erase them. The wilderness was teeming with people—people who took them in and heard them and shared their unorthodox ideas.

And so all these Asherahs are in obscurity. It's like there's an empty place where they used to be; you can tell something was there, but it's not clear. When you erase pencil lines, there are always ghostly impressions on the paper. Or when you close your eyes on a sunny day, you can see the bright shapes of trees or buildings inside your eyelids. Something was there, and now it's gone.

But you can see the absence. As her trees and high places were symbols of her presence, now her name is a symbol of all the others who are absent. Were they too sexual? Too black? Too fringe? Too convicting to those who saw them? Too frightening? Too different from the story we tell about ourselves? Or were they just wrong?

For me, considering Asherah isn't about rediscovering some ancient, perfect matriarchal society that the evil men destroyed. That didn't ever exist. And I'm not advocating for reintroducing a pagan (maybe not-so-pagan) goddess back into our everyday worship. I'm saying that her absence represents all that we excise because it is difficult, and specifically, all that we excise because it is female. I am actually sad that we've lost a lot of the feminine aspects of God. There are vestiges in scripture—Jesus describes God as a mother hen, and Paul compares the arc of history to a woman groaning in labor pains—but more often than not, God is "Father" and "husband" and "he." What's important to me is not whether Yahweh literally had a wife, but what that espousal suggests. If Asherah were intimately tied to Yahweh in something like a marriage, it's like an ancient version of the Trinity—not just that God is love but that in the end, God *is* community.

And Asherah's erasure makes me ask what else we've hidden and why. It's a metaphor for all of the things we'd rather other people didn't see, thank you very much. Churches hide sex scandals, politicians hide their true feelings and perform for the public, and parents hide vegetables in meatloaf. Keep in mind, hiding isn't necessarily bad. Oklahoma has the best, free preschool programs in the nation because the law creating them was hidden in the middle of completely different legislation, like vegetables in meatloaf. The point is, it's important to remember those who have gone before us, to know their stories, and to remind ourselves of what we've lost and why.

I am not being erased.

In my spiritual practice, Asherah's story is about being honest with myself about what I want to keep hidden. For years, I hid my towering rage from myself. My whole life, people asked me why I was so angry, to which I replied in a tense tone of voice, "I'm not angry." Oh, but I was, all the time, kind of like the Hulk. Because the world is so painfully broken and my little heart couldn't handle the sadness of what we do to each other, I got angry at all of it. But I thought that wasn't appropriate, which made me feel ashamed that I couldn't control my emotions. So I erased it from my consciousness. *I'm not angry, nope, not me.* Except the anger was still there, lying in wait, helping me to make my relationships messy and unpleasant. I had to see it in order to change it.

Asherah's story is also about transcending my story. That sounds kind of fancy. What I mean is that it has been easy to let myself be silent or even erased, to think that I am not important enough or that someone else's understanding of the story is more right than my own experience. I'm not a particularly quiet person, as my friends will attest, but I've allowed myself to fade into the background at times. I've ignored catcalling with my face burning and shame in my gut. I've pretended to myself that the experiences I've had don't stand up against someone else's. I will not be silent any longer.

I will not be absent. Humble perhaps, since I don't have all the answers. An intentional listener, absolutely. But I will be present.

Asherah's erasure reminds us to see things as they are, not as we want them to be. Her absence reminds us how important our presence is here and now.

Eve

Mother of All Living

Then the eyes of both were opened, and they knew that they were naked.

—GENESIS 3:7

First, there was nothing.

Or, rather, there was something, but it was chaos, a mess of light and dark and dry and wet and living and nonliving, and it was such a mess that it might as well have been nothing.

Before there was nothing, there was God. God moving over the deep mess of chaos. God breathing it in and out. God content and yet discontent. God wanting something instead of nothing.

So God made the world.

God pulled apart all the knotted strands of chaos and made mountains and rain and otters and cacti and swordfish and nebulae and people. The first story of creation we have says God made men and women at the same time. God looked at them and at all the something God had made and pronounced it very good. God brushed sand off the bum of the divine trousers and called it a day.

The second story of creation does things in a different order. It says God took that new dry land and made a person out of it, called it 'adamah in Hebrew, which means dirt or soil or earth. That makes sense. God's creature was genderless—a person made of mud. You might have called it earth-creature or earthling. And when God saw that the *'adamah* was lonely, God made the animals as companions. The *'adamah* liked the animals—thought the kittens were cute and the crocodiles terrifying and magnificent—but it was still lonely. So God put the *'adamah* to sleep and performed a bit of surgery, separating it into two people, then called *ish* and *ishah*, man and woman. They were helpers to each other. They lived in the garden called Eden and cared for it and for each other.

God said, as God often does in origin stories the world over, "You may eat anything in the garden I've made, anything at all, except from the tree of the knowledge of good and evil. If you do, you'll die, so just don't, okay?" And the *ish* and *ishah*, man and woman, said happily, "Sure thing, God," and went about their day.

Everything was lovely there in the garden called Eden. Everyone got along, there was plenty to eat, afternoons were lazy and restful, and everything was fine, just fine—for a time, anyway. Conflict always comes in these origin stories; it's one of the rules. Conflict came this time in the form of a serpent, a sneaky serpent who sneaked sneakily. It was clearly evil, bringing with it war and sexual immorality and embezzlement and someone eating the last cookie. Well, no, not exactly.

The woman was walking through the garden one day, carrying on her hip a basket full of fruits and vegetables she'd just picked. She passed under the shade of the tree of the knowledge of good and evil and was about to cross the little stream that ran by it when the sneaky serpent called to her. "Woman," it called, "wouldn't you like to harvest from this tree, too?" The woman said, "Of course not, silly. God told us to eat anything but that tree, or we'd die. Obviously, I wouldn't break that rule, would I?" She cocked her hip, the one supporting the basket, and took out a peach. She looked the serpent in the eye as she took a bite, and juice dripped down her chin.

The serpent knew a challenge when it heard one. It said, "That's ridiculous. You won't die. God said that because this tree, this particular tree, will open your eyes and you will see, well, you'll see everything. Just like God."

The woman took another bite of her peach and chewed it meditatively. She looked at the fruit of the tree of the knowledge of good and evil more closely. It looked ripe and delicious and harmless. And she did want to see everything. She put down her basket, and as the hero does in origin stories, she took one of the fruits and ate it. Her eyes were opened, and she became conscious of herself, of how beautiful the garden was, of how upset God would be when God found out, of how much more there was to know about the world. In essence, she grew up.

She called to the man. He came jogging around another path, and she became conscious of his body and her desire for it. Silently, she handed him the fruit of the tree of the knowledge of good and evil. He took it and looked at it, then at her. She nodded. He ate it. And he, too, saw the world around them with new eyes. He, too, grew up. At some point, all earth creatures see death and life, and we make the connection that other people are not us, that we are both separate selves and dependent on each other. It's not magic; it's just the way of things. The woman saw her own shock and joy on the man's face as his eyes widened and his breath came quicker. They stood directly in front of each other, not touching, just seeing for what felt like the first time. "We are in so much trouble," he said. "Yes," she said. "Will it be worth it?" he asked. "I don't know," she said. They picked up the basket and disappeared into the trees.

Later on, the story goes, God was walking in the garden at the time of the evening breeze. I love this image. It makes me smile to think that God, who once hovered over chaos, wanting something more, now had soft grass to walk on and pockets to put God's hands into and sunsets and gentle breezes to blow hair back from the divine forehead. God was walking in the garden. And God called to the man and the woman to join in the evening stroll, as they often did. They answered nervously from behind a hedgerow that they could not come out because they were naked.

God stopped. God looked at the hedgerow. God looked at the grass. God sighed.

"You ate from the tree, didn't you?" God asked, and a look crossed the face of God like—well, it looked like Ian McKellen in *The Lord of the Rings*. Man, he's good.

Remember that time at the council of Elrond when they were trying to figure out what to do with the evil One Ring? It had to be destroyed in Mordor, a horrifying, dangerous place a long journey away, and the big, powerful characters were arguing loudly about who should take it. Then Frodo, the very small, very charming hobbit who would prefer over all things to read and smoke his pipe, said quietly, "I will take the Ring to Mordor, though I do not know the way." As he said it, the camera rested on his mentor Gandalf's face, which did this simple thing: his eyes squeezed shut. Because of McKellen's subtlety, this one movement spoke of pride that Frodo had chosen to take the journey, relief that something had been decided, and grief at how much Frodo would lose because of his choice.

It was like that. The look that crossed God's face when the man and woman said they were naked was like that.

"What happened?" said God. The man faltered and said, "The woman—she gave it to me, and I ate it." The woman made a frustrated noise and said, "The serpent told me to eat it." The serpent said, "Yeah, I did. It's my role in the story as a change agent, so I did." God nodded slowly and turned to the man and woman. "This part of your story is over, then. You have sought knowledge and received it. Know, then, that you cannot stay here in this protected garden. Knowing what you do, knowing that you can hurt one another, you will. You can no longer be children playing in the dirt. You will have pain in childbirth and at work. Your children—your children will have pain, too, and you will not be able to prevent it. Go, my children, my beloved, go out into the world and make your way. And remember that you were sculpted from dirt, and to that dirt you will return."

Only then did they take names. The man became Adam, Man Made of Dirt. The woman became Eve, Mother of All Living.

Years later, after Eve had indeed had pain in childbirth twice over, her sons had grown and become farmers working the soil. Cain grew vegetables so flavorful and lovely they would make you weep, and Abel raised county-fair-prize-winning sheep. They took the first fruits of the garden and the firstborn lambs to their altar and sacrificed them to God, as they had been taught. And when God chose Abel's sheep offering over Cain's tomatoes and squash (who knows why), Cain grew angry. Cain murdered his brother and in so doing broke his mother's heart. Eve, Mother of All Living, was now also Mother of the Dead. Genesis doesn't speak of her grief because it's not important to the story, except that it is. Eve's grief over her son is pivotal to the story.

Eve's grief is our grief. We live in this world so very aware that we were sculpted from dirt and that we will eventually return to the dirt. Once we learn about death, everything we do is our response to knowing that. We are grieving our deaths by frantically building things and learning things and painting things and cooking things and pretending that we will get to keep doing those things when we, just like Abel, will die. And it breaks our hearts.

People say this story is about disobedience, and it absolutely is. God told Eve and Adam not to eat the fruit, and they did. It's about disobedience not because we needed to be punished, but because disobeying is what we do. It's about our desire for someone in authority to set rules for us to follow so we can feel good and right and proper when we follow them and also so we can break them. This, too, is how we grieve our deaths.

What it's not about is a legalistic give-and-take where God gave us a gift, and because we made a poor choice, we have lost everything forever and always. Usually, when Eve and Adam's story is told, it's about how innately terrible and self-interested we all are. St. Augustine called it original sin, lo these many years ago, and the name stuck. John Calvin went further and called it total depravity—that there is nothing good or salvageable in us. Now when we read it, we see proof of our guilt in the pain we feel in childbirth, in hard work, in brokenheartedness. If we are sad or angry or suffering, we must deserve it. But that's not what the story says, is it?

Around the time of Saint Augustine, there was this guy Pelagius, who read the same story and came out with something called original goodness. He said there was nothing evil in us but that we have collectively gotten into bad, self-interested habits. He was condemned as a heretic and exiled, his writings burned. From Pelagius, we might look at our suffering and reject any responsibility for it. But that's not what the story says either. Change, whether we judge it good or bad, is a normal and necessary part of the world unfolding.

The story is not about marriage being one man and one woman either. I don't mean that gender isn't important, but that's not the point of this story. It certainly is about marriage and partnership and reflects the dominant understanding of heterosexual marriage, but it emphasizes the partners' being one flesh, their being inseparable, their being balm to loneliness and help in difficulty.

Nor is it about women being the beginning of evil, being tempters and deceivers, being the source of men's sinful, sexual desire. That is the voice of control and of fear. I don't really know why we've got such a history of men refusing to hear women's voices or sharing power; that's a conversation for another book. But it is our history, going back to the first iterations of this story—a history that is beautiful and descriptive and also hurtful and proscriptive. The story has been used for centuries to keep women in our place in the kitchen and on our backs. But that's also not what it says, is it?

Reinterpreting this story is not about finding an easy way out. There isn't one. Eve's story doesn't tell us what to do with the knowledge of the world's complexity, only that it exists. We are not alone in our frustrations and pain and desire for our spouses; every other person on the planet and in history feels the weight of it. The creation stories in Genesis are stories of origin or cause—etiology, if you want to be fancy about it. They don't tell us how things ought to be but how they are. In the language of my seminary professors, they are not prescriptive but descriptive. It's an important distinction. Prescriptive stories use words like *should* and *ought* and *right* and *wrong*. Descriptive stories use, well, everything else.

These primordial stories cross cultures. They have rules that are supposed to be broken for them to be truthful. Breaking the rules is part of the story; otherwise, there is no story. Otherwise, there is no resonance with our lives. Eve is the seeker, the tester, the bringer of knowledge. She chooses to know and chooses to share what she knows. She doesn't give us a free pass out of our sin, but only shows us who we are and whose we are. Hers. And God's.

And now that we've gotten cosmic with the meanings of Eve's story, let me remind you that it's also small and domestic. This is what households look like: helping and caring for one another, blaming one another for problems, wondering what would happen if something changed. This is our experience of pain and frustration alongside knowing each other and the world. The story of creation is inseparably about epic changes and everyday life.

Saint Paul used this story to explain how important Jesus was. He said because we are all Adam and Eve's grandchildren, therefore we die. And since we are God's children because of Jesus the Christ, we will live. The truth of Eve's story lives on beyond her curiosity and heartbreak. The truth of Eve's story is that she is only the beginning.

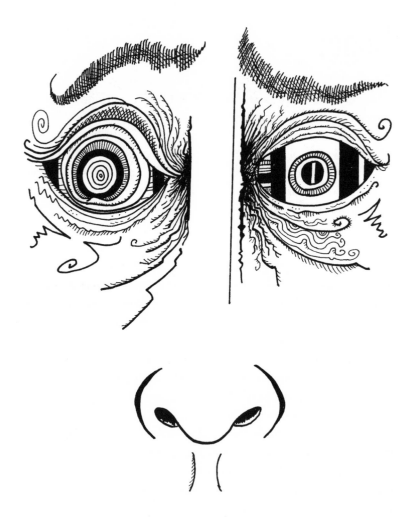

Hagar

Abraham's Other Woman

"Hagar, slave-girl of Sarai, where have you come from and where are you going?"

—GENESIS 16:8

Once upon a time, there were two people named Abraham and Sarah. Perhaps you've heard of them. They were the superstars of their day—larger than life, more faithful to God than anyone around, blessed with a miraculous child in their old age, the lead actors in the story everyone else was in. Think Paul Newman and Joanne Woodward. This was so long ago that dirt was a new concept. It was a time when the highs were high and the lows low—when all the stories told were epic.

Their story reminds me of the Psalms, actually, where the whole gamut of human experience is on display. The Psalmist speaks of overwhelming joy in God's presence and favor and turns around in a single verse and cries bitterly of abandonment. Abraham and Sarah's story swings from the mysticism of the first covenant, when in darkness a torch passed between halved animal carcasses, to the silliness of Sarah's laughter when she was told she'd have a baby at one hundred years old, to the terror of God commanding Isaac's sacrifice. Abraham and Sarah were like the great-grandparents of the American myth who came from the

Old World and built a cabin on the frontier with only a pen-knife and a magic bean, the stories they told filled with delight and heartbreak. In addition to all that, Abraham and Sarah were chosen by God and given not just *a* promise but *the* Promise: God would be with them always, their descendants would number as the stars, and they would be remembered unto ages of ages. This is the world of Abraham and Sarah.

But this is not their story. This is the story of one of the supporting actresses in their biblical blockbuster—or not even that, but an extra with a couple of lines. This is the story of Hagar.

Once upon a time, there was a woman named Hagar. Hagar was not a newspaper comic strip character—not a Viking warrior à la Hagar the Horrible. Hagar was Sarah's slave. She was a woman of little consequence, with no money, no family, no status at all. Like all women of her place and time, she was property, like a toaster oven or a family pet. She had no legal existence of her own, no recourse, no personal bank account. Yet she was happy, or as happy as could be expected. She was a part of a family—part of *the* family, really—not mistreated but useful and needed. She went about her daily life: doing the laundry, weaving and mending, helping with the farm, and shuttling the children of the camp to and from school, lacrosse, and band practice. It wasn't a bad life. But it wasn't *her* life.

Now, I don't want to fall into an assumption, in retelling this story, that slavery was and is somehow fine. I'm a white lady, and it would be easy to ignore the implications the black community sees in the story: that biblical slavery was used to justify the American slave trade, and that Sarah's mistreatment of Hagar looks an awful lot like how whites have treated blacks for centuries. Even worse, the story seems to imply that God is okay with all of that since God sends Hagar back into the situation. Culturally, Hagar's slavery was not like the centuries of Western Hemisphere slave trade, but neither was it morally superior. Hagar was property and treated as such, but she was herself before she was anyone else's.

The first hiccup came when Sarah, old and despairing of ever having a child of her own, said to Abraham, "It has ceased to be with me in the way of women" (at least that's what the King James translation tells us). "So I want you to take my slave Hagar and get her pregnant, and that child will be mine."

This kind of arrangement wasn't unheard of in those days. It was a little like when a woman's husband died and she married his brother, her children carrying on the name of the first husband, regardless who their daddy was. It's a little weird by modern standards, but wasn't back then. Abraham said, "Okay." (What, did you think he'd say no?) So they went to Hagar, and Sarah said, "It has ceased to be with me in the way of women, so I want you to get pregnant by my husband and give me the baby." Hagar knew this tradition and maybe half expected it to happen at some point—Sarah was getting up there in years, no matter what God had said in the Promise—but she also wasn't particularly thrilled. Being property, her consent was unnecessary, so Sarah's desire for a baby ended up feeling more than a little rape-y.

Abraham slept with Hagar, and she conceived a child. And even in the midst of the messy relationships, Hagar was as happy as could be expected. She was bringing life and prosperity to her family. She was pleased and proud to be needed and wanted and included. Her child would be Abraham and Sarah's, and now she was part of the Promise everyone talked about. Now she was really in with the "in" crowd. I imagine the first time she felt the baby move, it brought her to tears. She covered her mouth with one hand and her belly with the other as he pressed his hard foot up. There was life in this body, joy in this hard life.

But still the life was hard. Scripture says "she looked with contempt on her mistress." Maybe that was because, even though she was falling in love with the baby growing inside her, she still had the memory of Abraham groaning over her. Maybe because she wasn't allowed a life of her own. Maybe because she felt superior to Sarah—able to have a child and prove her worth as a woman, as Sarah couldn't. Sarah didn't take Hagar's contempt or her pregnancy well. She beat her every day and cursed her, saying, "You don't deserve my child in your womb, you filthy slave, you worthless dog!" Sarah, in her grief over being barren, in her pain over watching Hagar's growing belly, drove Hagar into the desert to die. After all they'd done, she rejected even this slim hope of the Promise being real.

In the desert, pregnant and alone, Hagar cried. She cursed Sarah. She despaired. And she met God—I mean really met God. In those days of epic struggles, God walked among the people. In the desert, God appeared by Hagar's side and spoke to her. God saw her misfortune, and God saw *her*. In the desert, where Hagar had lost all hope, God gave her a promise, too. Her children would one day number as the stars, and she would be the matriarch of a great nation.

And Hagar—this unknown, inconsequential slave girl—named God. She gave God not a title or a description but a name, becoming the only person in the Bible to do so. *El-roi* she called God: "God who sees."

Hagar returned to the camp and to her adopted family, rejoicing in the divine knowledge that she was truly a part of the Promise, her face glowing from her encounter with God. She also felt fear as she returned. What awaited her in the camp? What would Sarah do? We are left wondering, too, because the writers of Genesis aren't interested.

The story skips ahead some years, to when strangers came into the camp, proclaiming that Sarah would become great with child, and she laughed. Nervously? Deeply and heartily? Knowing what she had done and lost? Either way, it came to pass that she was once again in the way of women, and she became great with child.

As amazing and wonderful as it was, I imagine Sarah was scared. I sure was, and I wasn't, like, ninety when I got pregnant the first time. She knew so many women who hadn't survived childbirth even when they were young and healthy. Sarah needed advice, someone to talk to. The text doesn't say that they found common ground, but I'll bet Sarah screwed up her courage and went to Hagar, her slave whom she had scorned and beaten and driven away. Maybe Hagar met her at the entrance to her tent and looked at her with questions in her eyes. Maybe things were different now and soon they were weeping and laughing together. They would have talked about their aches and pains, their hunger, their deep connection with their babies. They would have discussed birthing plans and breathing techniques and prenatal yoga.

When Hagar gave birth, she named her son Ishmael after the narrator of *Moby-Dick*. When Sarah gave birth, she named her son Isaac after the ancient Middle Eastern violinist Itzhak Perlman. And Sarah looked upon the child of her slave . . . and she hated him. She said, "My Isaac will not grow up playing with the help." She went to Abraham and said, "Abe, my Isaac will not grow up playing with the help. Her Ishmael will not have part of our property or our promise. He's not really our child, you know, and Hagar, she's only a slave. Get rid of them." Things weren't different, as it turned out. Their relationship was still deeply broken, and Hagar's joy was about to turn to misery.

Abraham looked out into the yard at Ishmael his firstborn son and at Isaac his miraculous child. I believe he loved those boys, but like tragic heroes the world over, he was not perfect. Abraham loved his sons, and he made a terrible decision to go along with Sarah's jealousy. Abraham turned Hagar and his own son out into the desert with only a loaf of bread and a single bottle of water. Hagar looked him in the eye before he turned back. "I see you, the real you," she thought. "I know what you're doing. Do you know what you're doing?"

Out in the desert again, Hagar was alone, unmourned, and unloved, a secondary character in a made-for-TV movie. She raised her hands to the empty sky and screamed, "Where are you now, God, and where is your Promise?" All she could think of was the look of triumph on Sarah's face. Even her friends in the camp had turned away from her shame. Her family had kicked her out like a dog because of who she was, what she'd done and said and seen. She wandered the wilderness, knowing this time she couldn't go back. There were no friendly faces, no street signs, not even a trickling stream. Hagar wandered, carrying her toddler son and the bottle of water—the one getting heavier, the other getting lighter—her heart breaking.

And her eyes were opened, and behold, she knew they could not survive on their own. So she laid Ishmael under a bush, not able to watch her own son die of starvation, and she stumbled away, hot tears streaming down her face. She lifted up her voice with her son's and wailed with *no one* to hear.

But God heard. God heard her cries and joined her there in the wilderness. God sat with her, suffered with her, a few hard paces from her squalling baby boy. And God mourned with her for all she had lost. God reminded her of the Promise she already had: "You will never be alone. I will be with you. I will make you the matriarch of a great nation, too, and you will be remembered unto ages of ages. There is light here in the midst of your darkness. There is hope here in the midst of your wilderness." God showed her a well in the desert, and she drank deep.

Hagar's wilderness is our wilderness. We wander out here, feeling abandoned and rejected, protecting our wounded selves. It feels like there are no friendly faces, no street signs, not even a trickling stream. I have a colleague whose parents kicked them out because they identified as a lesbian and later as trans. They were on their own at the age of sixteen, unloved and hardened. They are now happily married and successful—they even have made peace with their parents—but they carry that piece of wilderness with them. God was with them in that misery. God saw them, sat with them, showed them the well in the wilderness.

I am an angry person; anything from stubbing my toe to hateful political rhetoric can set off a burning fire of anger in my belly. But it turns out that anger is really just a protective measure I've developed to hide how sad I am. And recently, I've been very sad. I feel the tears well up while I'm cooking or writing or looking at the trees from my back porch. Thinking about how hateful we humans are to each other will do it, but it's the closer-to-home stuff that makes my chest ache. Thinking about my daughter's neighborhood friends rejecting her, as kids do when they're experimenting with how to do relationships, opens the floodgates. People's misunderstanding of who I am hurts. A friend once called me "whimsical," which is a nice way to say people think I'm superweird. I have strong opinions about how to do and be church, how to accept all kinds of people as they are, and I act on them. It feels perfectly normal to me, not weird at all. But those opinions are not necessarily what other people think, and their hesitation, even their legitimate criticisms, feel like a rejection of my whole self. I carry a piece of wilderness with me. And God is with me, already acting in that wilderness. God sees me, sits with me, patiently shows me the well.

Christian community at its best is both broken—because it's made up of all of us broken, wandering people—and hopeful. Our meal at the table every week in the middle of worship is our way of feeding each other in the wilderness. It's our way of lighting the darkness. It's our way of seeing God and reminding each other that God sees us, too.

Hagar named God El-roi, "the God who sees." And God heard her cries in the wilderness: "the God who hears." And God came to her side and sat next to her while she wept: "the God who sits." God does not leave Hagar or Ishmael or Sarah or Isaac or us: "God who is with us," *Emmanuel.*

God sees, God hears, God is with us.

Deborah and Jael

Women on Top

Barak said to Deborah, "If you will go with me, I will go; but if you will not go with me, I will not go."

And she said, "I will surely go with you; nevertheless, the road on which you are going will not lead to your glory, for the Lord will sell Sisera into the hand of a woman."

Then Deborah got up and went with Barak to Kedesh.

—JUDGES 4:8–9

A long time ago, there were judges in Israel. This was before there were kings but after God had created the world, you understand, so the judges were not as domesticated as Solomon or David, but they were mighty to behold. The judges in Israel—they were like divinely appointed warlords, leaders of the tribes of Israel while they were still new to being a nation, still enamored of their past as conquering heroes and glorious slaughterers of the Canaanites. Well, they'd intended to slaughter them gloriously, but you know, slaughtering is hard work, and somewhere along the line, they just settled down in Canaan and married them. They also started worshipping the Canaanite gods Baal and Asherah. They were, the book of Judges constantly reminds us, evil in the sight of the Lord, so God let them be invaded and oppressed by a long succession of other nations.

The judges in Israel tried to get the Israelites to stop being so damn evil in the sight of the Lord, to minimal success. Mostly, their stories are colorful anecdotes (and by "colorful," I mean graphic and gross). Sampson was a judge—all raw power and hair he was. He ripped a lion into pieces with his bare hands and later ate honey from a beehive that had formed in the lion's carcass. He killed a thousand men with the jawbone of an ass. He was oddly gullible when his lover Delilah said, "You're so strong, baby, but I bet there's a way to make you weak. What is it, boo?" Three times she asked, and then she used the information to betray him. (To be fair to Delilah, the Philistines had threatened to burn her and her family alive if she didn't help them, so there's that.)

Gideon was famous for triumphantly tearing down a shrine to Baal and Asherah, though he did it in the middle of the night because he was afraid of what the people would do to him. So he was a little less triumphant than he intended. And Jephthah—ah, Jephthah. He was a soldier's soldier, that one—a great warrior whose family made fun of him for being the son of a whore. He only led the armies of Israel to prove to them he was worth more than anyone had bargained for. If only he hadn't made a fool's bargain and sacrificed his daughter for a military victory. But of all these and many more, the greatest was Deborah.

Deborah was married to a man named Lappidoh, which means "spirited" or "fiery" or "fierce." Or else Lappidoh was a nickname meaning "spirited" or "fiery" or "fierce." No one really knew. Deborah the Wife of Ferocity sat under a tree at the outskirts of town and was a judge for the people. She sat under a tree, which came to be known as Deborah's Tree, and listened to their stories. *Whose cow is this legally? What do I do when my husband beats me? How do we observe the Sabbath in our hearts as well as our homes?* Deborah saw the breath of God in each person, saw the truth of their hearts. She sat there under her tree and saw the blue of the sky and the clouds, like paste, scraping across it. She sat, watching, listening, advising. And she heard the voice of God.

One day she called the general of the Israelite army to her. As she watched him come, she saw his passions and his faults. "General Barak," said Deborah the Wife of Ferocity, "God has a word to speak to you. God says to get your army in gear and go to Mount Tabor and fight the horde of the Great and Terrible General Sisera. God says you will fight and you will win."

General Barak said to Deborah, "Will you come with me?" for he was brave, but not as brave as Deborah the Wife of Ferocity. "If you go with me," he said, "I will go. But if you do not, I will not go." And General Barak hung his head and traced circles in the dirt with his foot like a little boy.

Deborah looked at Barak and knew his heart, and she sighed. Deborah said, "I will indeed go with you, General Barak, but you'd better get ready for disappointment. You'll win, but it won't be because of you. Triumph will belong to a woman. You got that?"

So they went to the battlefield with their scant ten thousand soldiers, and behold, there was Sisera and all his massive army with nine hundred iron chariots, an overwhelming sight. Barak might have wished to be the man stabbed in the toilet rather than be here, it was so frightening. Think of the climactic battle of *Lord of the Rings* at Pelennor Fields, only with fewer trolls and orcs. And the Israelites looked over the army of Sisera and were afraid.

But Deborah the Wife of Ferocity said to General Barak, "Get up! God is giving Sisera and all his army into your hand. God is your front line and your rear guard. Go, fight, win!"

So they marched forward and saw Sisera's army, and Sisera's army saw them. They watched each other, saw how many soldiers were on each side, and saw that the God of Israel was indeed with Israel. And Sisera's army panicked—horses rearing and trampling, soldiers fleeing, glorious iron chariots crushing bodies, and no officers able to form order. The Great and Terrible General Sisera was seen leaping from his own chariot and running away on foot like a scaredy-cat.

Deborah the Wife of Ferocity may or may not have rolled her eyes.

Suddenly General Barak had the courage of his convictions and called to his small army to pursue the great host of Sisera's army and cut them down. They pursued Sisera's army all the way back to Harosheth-ha-goiim—which might mean Sisera's Hometown or Foreigners We Beat in Battle or maybe So Many Dead. Every last warrior of the enemies of Israel died by the sword of Barak's army.

Deborah the Wife of Ferocity may or may not have had a gleam in her eyes.

Now, you may well think that the glory of this story belongs to Deborah, the warrior-woman judge. But there's more.

Sisera himself, Great and Terrible General of the Bad Guy Army, had escaped the wholesale slaughter of his troops. He'd run away with his tail between his legs toward the tent city Elon-bezaanannim, which means something fascinating about an oak tree we don't know how to translate. The Kenites lived there—distant, distant cousins of the Israelites, so distant that they weren't on speaking terms. Well, you know how it is, you don't talk for years, then you get together, and it's just like old times, and you share all your metalworking and art-making skills with each other. It was like that between the Kenites and the Israelites. Anyway, Sisera the Great and Terrible ran away to this tent city at Elon-bezaanannim because he knew they were still on his side, hoping to hide himself in their midst.

"Pssst," he heard, and he looked and saw a woman gesturing him into her tent. In relief, Sisera snuck into the darkness.

Jael was the woman's name, and she had been sitting at the entrance to her tent, watching and waiting. She sat there and saw the blue of the sky and the clouds, like paste, scraping across it. She sat there in front of the tent and saw her people's allies run away and fall by her enemies' swords. Did she hear the voice of God telling her Sisera was coming? Did she think she could protect herself and her family by changing sides? Why did she wait for this man, and for what? No one knew.

Jael was married to a man named Heber. His name might also have meant Ferocity for all we know, because here is what she did. Sisera the Great and Terrible was also Sisera the Fearful and Exhausted, so he asked for some water. Jael instead gave him fresh milk to slake his thirst, like your mother might have given you before you went to bed, a soothing gesture.

Sisera may or may not have noticed the nuance as he drank the milk down. His exhaustion hit him, and he thought, "I'll sort this Barak and Deborah thing out tomorrow when I'm rested," and he lay down to sleep. Just before falling asleep in the tent of this obviously trustworthy and tasteful woman, Sisera told her to lie if anyone asked if he were there.

As his eyes drifted closed, Jael the wife of Heber picked up a tent peg. She picked up a hammer. She laid the tent peg against Sisera's lips and gave it such a mighty blow with the hammer that it pierced Sisera's spine and lodged in the ground beneath his head.

And Jael the Wife of Ferocity went outside her tent to wait for whomever would come. And she might or might not have pondered all the deeds of Sisera that had led her to this moment.

Barak the Newly Great and Terrible came into the Kenite camp, and Jael rose to meet him. She said, "Come into my tent"—a terrifying statement if you know what's inside. But Barak didn't know, and he went and saw his enemy nailed to the ground. Barak might or might not have marveled at the deeds of women.

He also might or might not have thrown up.

In nearby Harosheth-ha-goiim, General Sisera's mother sat at the entrance to her tent, watching and waiting. She sat there and saw the blue of the sky. She sat there and saw the blue of the sky and the clouds, like paste, scraping across it. She sat there in front of the tent and saw the people coming, and she wondered aloud how the battle was going for her son and his troops. To the other women sitting in front of their tents, she asked, "Where could they be? Those iron chariots they built should have made short work of the Israelites." The other mothers and sisters and wives sat silently, looking out at the horizon, willing the men to return. Sisera's mother answered her own question, "Surely they are taking so long because there was so much to plunder in the Israelite camp, so many women to rape and slaughter for birthing those filthy Israelites, so many riches to carry back to us." She could have been called the Wife of Ferocity herself. Yet how she and the other mothers and sisters and wives would weep for their men, how they would grieve their protectors and lovers and grown children.

Deborah and Jael, the wives of Ferocity, the wives of Necessity and of Wisdom, lived, if not happily ever after, then content, aware of the parts they had played in the great story God was telling with Israel.

Of course, it's not that simple. In war, no one lives happily ever after; no one is content, least of all the women. Even the victors, the Israelites, couldn't have had an unambiguously joyful celebration. They had their own dead to bury, their own wounds to bind. They continued to do what was right in their own eyes—to take from their neighbors and to pretend they didn't need God. They were oppressed again and again, whether we believe God willed it or not. They, like us, weren't so much punished for their sins as punished by them.

Deborah and Jael might be role models for us to fan the flames of our own ferocity, to make things right and protect our own, but they might simply be part of us, a description of what we feel and do. I don't want to murder someone with a tent peg, but the feeling is there whether I want it or not. If I think about someone hurting or taking my children, the fire rises inside my belly, choking me with rage: "You will not touch them; you will suffer if you do." If I wonder very long about the motivations of people who neglect or molest foster children, I feel that fire rising again. When I see how we treat the creation God has made for us, the fire burns hotter. When I see how I hurt people around me with criticism and this burning anger, the fire turns to a coal that burns me from the inside out. It simmers in my belly, waiting for its moment to explode. How could we treat each other as we do? How can we be so selfish and violent? It makes me want to break something. Ironic, I know.

Maybe this is the quandary the wives of Ferocity felt—their desire to fix things and their desire to protect. I wonder how Jesus sees this inner fire, given his words about forgiveness and his own anger in the temple and at the fig tree. Are Deborah and Jael not only describing our capacity for ferocity but also our capacity for contemplation? I really want to offer you a clear, neat way to understand these warrior women and to take them into your souls. But they're difficult and violent, and the Bible itself affirms their violence. They did watch and wait, but they weren't peaceful contemplatives. They were human and heroic and ambiguous.

Deborah and Jael live on in Afghanistan, where women teach their children history and faith and how to protect their families, and teenagers open schools for girls, in defiance of the Taliban. They live on in India, where women fight off rapists on buses. They live on in Kenya, where women plant trees in defiance of the government's edict that women aren't allowed to and the trees won't make any difference anyway. Deborah and Jael live on in small-town America, where women run for school board and city council and mayor and stare down those who would question their authority to change things. They live on in our prayer life and our attempts to see the world as it is, rather than as we want it to be. Deborah and Jael live on in us when we call upon our own ferocity to see the breath of God in each person, to see their passions and their faults. When we sit, watching, listening, and waiting, we, too, might hear the voice of God.

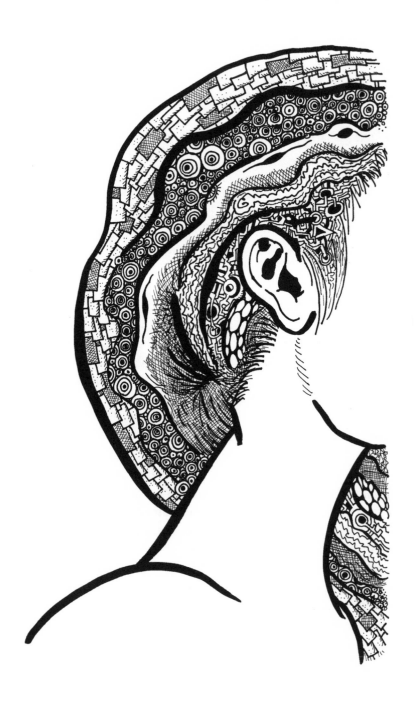

Song of Songs

The Sexy, Sexy Bible

How fair and pleasant you are,
    O loved one, delectable maiden!
You are stately as a palm tree,
    and your breasts are like its clusters.
I say I will climb the palm tree
    and lay hold of its branches.
O may your breasts be like clusters of the vine,
    and the scent of your breath like apples,
and your kisses like the best wine
    that goes down smoothly,
    gliding over lips and teeth.

—Song of Songs 7:6–9

For several centuries, Christians have tried to figure out what the hell the Song of Songs is about. Now, if you were to go read it, you might say to yourself, "What's the question again? Isn't it about sex?" Yes, yes it is.

Christians are weird about sex. It's obviously something most of us do, but we don't talk about it much, except maybe to accuse someone else of doing it wrong. Twenty-first-century American Christianity is known for not being much fun in the bedroom. But here in the middle of the Bible is a long poem about two

89

people's very physical love for each other. It's awkward. Why is it even there?

First thing is, it's poetry; it means more than it seems to mean. Like the TV show *Lost*, or the songs of Radiohead, or any of Frida Kahlo's paintings. Only better. For a long time, people called it "Song of Solomon" under the assumption that King Solomon was also a masterful poet. But the title in Hebrew is "Song of Songs" and means it's the best, the most beautiful of all the songs. It's early Hebrew erotica but with complex meaning in addition to breasts.

Some people see the Song of Songs as a kind of performance art, reenacting a fertility rite to bring good harvest. Other people see it as an allegory—a one-to-one metaphor about God's love for noncompliant Israel. My friend Rabbi Yitz says Jews read it on the feast of Passover, which is about God dating and ultimately marrying Israel under the canopy of clouds at Mount Sinai. Similarly, in some Christian thought, it's about God dating the church. Others see it literally as a celebration of sex and romance, both gifts from God. Still others wonder why it's in the Bible at all, since God's not mentioned in it once.

We don't read it in church much. Catholic, Episcopal, Lutheran, and other liturgical churches use a three-year schedule of Bible readings for Sunday worship called a lectionary. That schedule doesn't include the Song of Songs at all. You might hear it at a wedding here and there, but only the least racy parts—like, not the bits with dripping nard or "channels" or bellies and breasts and lips. That stuff is best kept far away from Sunday morning. Only, why? Are we embarrassed? And of what? That sex exists at all or that *we* have it? And think about it. A lot. What people's bodies do isn't really a surprise. When we baptize a baby into the faith on a Sunday morning, we know someone's genitals were involved in making that baby. But we don't talk about *those* in church, even though they play a starring role in tons of Bible stories—and our own thoughts.

The Bible is R-rated, you know. Wide swaths of it aren't translated accurately because the Hebrew or Greek is too coarse. Every time in Genesis when someone uncovers someone else's feet, it means genitals. Sometimes men swear by putting their hands on each other's thighs, and by "thighs," they mean penises. Violence in the form of genocide, rape, and disfigurement is common. Ezekiel, bless him, is foul no matter how you translate him, but literal translations would make your ears burn.

The Song of Songs is about a woman who is deeply in love and lust with her beloved, who may or may not be King Solomon. Probably not. And they have frequent trysts but apparently don't live together. Or maybe they're married, though the text doesn't offer much support for that. Or maybe their relationship is scandalous somehow, since she gets beaten at one point for trying to find him. The poem is not a straightforward story with a beginning, middle, and end, nor is it entirely clear who the characters are. It reads a bit like a series of monologues between the man and the woman, but they don't always flow from one to another.

The language, as you might expect, is heightened, is metaphorical: "your teeth are like a flock of goats"; "your neck is like a tower, all its stones in courses." It's like saying, "Your skin is as soft as a kitten's fur" or "Your hips are as curvaceous as the Guggenheim Museum, and truly, they don't lie." Her neck is not a tower, not really, and her teeth aren't hairy like a flock of goats. It's about taking inspiration from the natural and human-made world: What's beautiful to you? That's what you compare your love to. Among other things, I find concrete walls that have been graffitied and then painted over with various overlapping neutral paint to be beautiful. So I might say to my husband, "Your mind is lovely, lovelier than repainted concrete walls, deeper than many layers of paint." Or maybe I wouldn't say that, exactly. You get the point.

"Your body," the woman says in one place, "is like ivory." The Hebrew word translated "body" means a man's midsection, but not his stomach muscles or hips. She is saying the man's penis is like ivory, hard and long like an elephant's tusk. Yes, in a lovely, poetic way, she's saying, "my beloved is well hung."

Even without such translations, the Bible is all about violence and strong language and adult situations. It's not for the faint of heart, because our lives are not for the faint of heart. The stories in it can speak to us on the level they do *because* they reflect our own violence and strong language and adult situations. As we used to say in seminary, it's not prescriptive (telling us to go do something particular), it's descriptive (showing us what we look like). It's about recognition and awareness, maybe a little longing for things to be different. The Song of Songs holds up a mirror and says, "Isn't this physical love we have wonderful? Isn't it hard sometimes, too? Don't you see your own relationship here? And maybe your love of God here, too?" The Song of Songs, arguably more than the rest of the Bible, is about seeing the truth of our selves, unvarnished and vulnerable in our nakedness.

I mentioned earlier that some folks read the Song of Songs as a metaphor for God dating the church. It's a theology called "bridal mysticism," which dates back to the early church and describes Jesus as our collective and individual boyfriend. Basically, when we are united with God, it's a bit (or a lot) like getting married, complete with physical intimacy. Yes, that inappropriate image in your head is exactly what I'm talking about. If you think of it literally, it's a bit creepy. But it's also beautiful. We see married people all the time; certainly we see broken marriages, but we also see connectedness and reliance and forgiveness. Why wouldn't we use that as a metaphor for our relationship with God? Bridal mysticism takes Jesus as the boyfriend to its logical extreme and puts the mystic or the reader in the place of the bride. When we read these passages, when we pray to God, we can experience the great hope a bride feels—the anticipation of new life, the excitement of being with the one our heart most desires.

You know this feeling. Not just the heart palpitations of a crush, but the deep connectedness to someone you truly love and who loves you back. For some, that might be a romantic or married partner; for others, it might be a deep soulfriend; for others, it could be the relationship you have with a parent or sibling. These are beautiful experiences, and they require a certain vulnerability on our end. To the extent that we allow our real, inner selves to be seen, we are loved all the more. In the same way, we have to be able to be vulnerable to God. Bridal mysticism requires us to present ourselves exactly as we are to our bridegroom, Jesus.

The Song of Songs is scandalously specific and also ambiguous. It is almost pornographic and deeply spiritual. The Song of Songs is about sustaining relationships and about constantly striving, and it is about the love that is the ground of all our being in one way or another. Which is lovely and complex and all that, but it's also direct. The narrator of the Song of Songs is the only woman in scripture who tells her own story. Every other woman's story is told by someone else, either by another character in a story or by the writer of the book she appears in. Here, the woman speaks in the first person; she is a woman in touch with her own heart and mind, a woman in touch with her sensuality, a woman empowered. She is her own person as well as the man's lover.

She was told she had to work in her brothers' vineyards. She was told she had dark, ugly, black skin. She was told she'd never amount to anything, that she was unlovable. She was told she would have babies, and that would make her valuable. She was told to be quiet in church, to submit to her husband, to lie back and think of England. She was told it was all in her head, that it was her fault. She was told.

And now she will tell.

When she saw him the first time, she came over, all giddy. She was talking to her friend, and suddenly she was stammering, and her hands were shaking, and her nipples got hard, and she couldn't stop staring. When he talked to her the first time, she looked down at her shaking knees, knowing he couldn't possibly find her pleasant to look at, but he lifted her chin with a finger and looked at her as no one else ever had. It felt as if he actually saw her—her self, her soul, the woman that she knew so well but that she protected. What did he see in her?

He said that she was more beautiful than a flock of goats on the hillside, sweeter than persimmons dipped in honey, more elegant than the Temple Mount itself. He said, "She's a brick house!" He compared her breasts to round baby sheep nursing at their mother's side. He said her heart was bigger than the Jerusalem marketplace, that her mind was sharper than the rocks at the shore that tear up the hulls of boats, that her ass was as round as melons and how he wanted to take a bite.

How could he see all this when she was, at best, average? He saw her, and he loved her. And she saw him, and she loved him.

They devour each other with their eyes. When they see each other around town, from yards and yards away, they cannot resist seeing, they cannot resist knowing. They know that last night they spoke of philosophy and the nature of God, they spoke of politics and farming and birds and bees, and they spoke of their fears and of their darkest fantasies. And they touched each other. They removed each other's clothes slowly, achingly slowly, fingers tracing the hollow of the throat like the curve of a spoon dipped in custard, fingers circling wrists vulnerable as new leek shoots, fingers caressing inner thighs open like a book revealing its secrets. And today, when they see each other, they know, deeply, what the other looks like under their clothes, how the other responds to kisses, and what the other looks like right after. They devour each other with more than their eyes.

Yet she cannot see him now. And so often, she cannot find him. He doesn't respond when she calls, and her friends have not seen him. She runs across sidewalks and fields, through the autumn trees smelling of wet leaves and death, and she weeps. She meets people as she wanders, and they look at her in disgust. They speak harshly, telling her no one could love her as he does, telling her she's making a fool of herself, telling her to not to speak up for herself, telling her to go home.

So she returns to her bed, to her empty apartment, which still smells of his soap and his skin and sex. She returns to her shower and washes away her tears in hot water. She rubs lotion into her skin and puts on her pajamas, giving in to exhaustion. She tells herself it will be better tomorrow. She tells herself he will return. She tells herself to fall asleep. She gives in to memories and touches herself. And just on the edge of sleep, she thinks she hears him next to her, his hand on her belly, his lips at her ear. She wakes with a jolt, but he is not there. She runs to the door, her hands still slick with lotion and her own moisture, her feet bare, but he is not there. The hall is empty; the street is empty; her heart is full. Where is her love? What shall she do with the fullness of her heart in this empty world?

Later, when she has found him again, they have carved out time to lie on the grass, feeling the warm sun on their skin, seeing the red glow of it through their eyelids, smelling burning leaves and each other's familiar scent. Cloves and eucalyptus and nard fill her nose and her heart. His hand is in hers, their only touchpoint, yet containing multitudes. She basks in her beloved's presence, and he in hers.

She tells him all the skeptics cannot quench their love. Many insults will not quench her joy in her own body nor the want she feels for him, her beloved. Their sorrows and arguments will not quench their commitment. Many wars cannot quench the spark of the divine and the hope of peace. Many waters cannot quench the fire of her love; neither can floods drown it.

Listen, whether Jesus is your boyfriend or your husband or a casual friend, whether your sexual life is passionate or nonexistent, may this woman's words wash over you and ignite the coals in your soul. May the Song of Songs turn you on to someone who will love you as you are. May it turn you on to something that makes your body ache to learn more. May you be overcome with excitement and run into the streets heedless of others' scorn. May you fall in love with the life that God has given you, and may you feel God embracing and supporting you every moment of your life.

Widows

Those Left Behind

Do no wrong or violence to the alien, the orphan, and the widow, nor shed innocent blood in this place.

—JEREMIAH 22:3B

At a church service recently, I sat behind my good friends Mark and Jill. As we listened to the sermon, I watched as she lay her arm over the back of the chair and slowly rubbed his shoulder with her hand. I thought, "She knows where all his moles are, which muscles are the most painful after a marathon, what his breathing sounds like when he's sick." And I thought, "That is such a gift." They've been married for years and years, and the love they share has evolved and deepened. Her hand moving over his back spoke of that love and of comfort and familiarity.

Watching this brief, casual moment reminded me of my own marriage and the knowing we share. We have been married for seventeen years and together for twenty, as of this writing, and I know his moles and muscles and breathing as he knows mine. There's a peace in knowing someone else's body as you know your own, and in knowing someone else's mind as you know their body—not reading that person's mind, but knowing it the way you know the creases worn into soft skin.

What must it be like to lose that familiarity? To wake up expecting your partner to be there next to you as he or she always is, snoring away or cover-stealing, and to find yourself alone again?

I don't do well when my husband is just out of the city. I mean, I'm a functional adult, so I get the kids dressed and go to work and everything; it's not like I fall apart. But the dishes pile up. And my creative projects lose some of their spark. And slouching on the couch and watching British cooking shows all night seems like an excellent idea. When he's here, I get shit done. It's not like I need a man to get that shit done; I need my partner—the other half of our unit, the other half of our *ha-adam*, the Earth Creature that God made us to be. It's hard to be alone when you're used to someone else's body being around. But I'm not a widow, so I only have a glimpse.

There was a widow who lived in Zarephath whose only family was her son and whose only food was a little flour and oil. There was a drought on, you see, so all the people around were suffering. We don't know any more about her than that. Was she a young widow with a toddler son? Was she quite old, and her son was grown? How did her husband die? We only know she was poor and, because she was a widow, was without protection. When the famous prophet Elijah passed through town, he saw her collecting sticks. He said, "Woman, bring me some water. And some food as well. For God—my God and your God—has said you will feed me." I'm not kidding; that's what he said. Typical. She paused in her stick gathering and said, "Sir, I would be happy to help you out on any other day than today. I have so little to eat that my son and I are just now going to go eat it and then die of starvation." Elijah, undeterred, said, "It will not run out. Go and make some little pancakes with the flour and oil, and bring me some. You'll see what God can do."

Seeing that she was planning to die anyhow, the widow shrugged and did what he said. She poured out the little flour she had into a bowl, mixed the last of the oil with it, and poured it onto a griddle. As it browned around the edges, she thought of all the times she'd made these cakes for her husband, all the times he'd embraced her, all the times they'd laughed and argued in this room. Her chest felt tight, so she put her shoulders back and took a deep breath, her eyes wet but not overflowing. She took a pancake to the prophet and returned home to await death with her son.

Her eye caught on the empty jar of flour. Which wasn't empty. She snatched up the bottle of oil. Also not empty. How could this be? For days and days afterwards, the widow of Zarephath was able to feed herself, her son, and the prophet Elijah, who had brought them possibility.

Another story goes that the widow of Zarephath's son died. Her only family, her only possibility of future support was gone. Her boy, who had made her laugh as much as he made her want to scream. Her boy, whom she had carried in her belly and then in her arms. She confronted Elijah, saying, "You saved our lives during the drought only for him to die now? What kind of prophet of the Lord are you?" And Elijah, good man that he was, said to her, "I got this." He went to the boy's room and lay on top of him. Yes, he lay himself on top of the corpse; it's how God works sometimes, mysteriously, weirdly. That's not the point. The point is that Elijah, prophet of the Lord, a very important person, cared for this widow in Zarephath enough to bring her family back to life.

There's a similar story in Luke about a widow from Nain. Jesus was walking down the road—the dude rarely was in a town or a home, always walking somewhere, always out where the people were—and he saw a funeral procession. The pallbearers carried a young man among them, and behind was a woman weeping. Somehow he knew she was a widow—I mean, he's Jesus, so of course he did—and that this was her only son. She was alone in the world. Jesus couldn't abide that. He had compassion for her, the text says, so he went to the pallbearers, put his hand on the dead boy's leg, and said, "Stand up, son. Your mama misses you." And he did.

There are so many others. Anna was eighty-four when she met the baby Jesus. She'd been a widow for maybe sixty years, and there near the end of her life, she was known as a prophet and a woman of great faith. With her elderly friend Simeon, she was given the chance to see the Messiah, to hold him in her arms and tickle his tiny toes and know that everything would be okay in the end. Naomi, Ruth's mother-in-law, was a widow. Eunice and Lois, mother and grandmother of Paul's friend Timothy, were widows. The story of the "widow's mite" is often told in churches, holding up this woman and her extreme generosity (she gave everything she had, people!), but others see it as Jesus shaming the establishment (she gave everything she had, people—how are you going to respond?).

Widows in the ancient Middle East had to fend for themselves. Because a woman was considered property (bought and sold in marriage for livestock and trade agreements), once her husband died, she had no one required to take care of her—no one around to worry for her health or to inspire her work. Ideally, she would have had many children who grew up hale and hearty, who would take her in, but that didn't always happen. All throughout the law and the prophets, the writers remind us to protect widows and orphans and foreigners. James says that in order to be "doers of the word," we have to care for orphans and widows. Israel as a whole is blamed for natural and national disasters because they did not follow through on those protections. Because widows (and orphans and foreigners) are stand-ins for everyone who is helpless and hopeless, they are themselves in need of care, and they are symbols of our unwillingness to look beyond our own noses.

The widows are also examples of good, Christian behavior, according to the letter to Titus. They are teachers of the younger generation, holding within themselves not only what is right, but also what is beautiful. They are wise, and they are alone. And at least in scripture, we never hear about their internal lives. Widows appear everywhere in scripture: quick mentions you don't even notice as you pass by, eager for the meat of the story, or as central characters in stories that are about something else entirely.

One Sunday at the church I service, I was distributing Communion bread, saying, "Receive what you are, the body of Christ." I stepped forward to a new row of people kneeling at the altar rail and saw Mary, a widow in the church, supporting the arm of an older lady next to her. She'd helped this other woman walk down the aisle to the rail. Watching them, I remembered a recent conversation with Mary when she'd said, "I love spending time with the older folks. They have such wonderful stories. It really fills my heart." I looked at her at the altar rail, and I thought, "Mary, you *are* the older folks. How long until someone is supporting your arm as you come forward for Communion?" I should be clear that Mary is unbelievably vital and engaged. She won't slow down for years and years yet. But slow down she will, as will all of us. Thinking of her being supported on her way to Communion made me tear up. I had to swallow hard to be able to say, "Receive what you are, the body of Christ," to the next person.

Mary's husband, Dave, was by all accounts a damned fine man. He was inquisitive, a good listener, super-smart, and he loved to play devil's advocate. Mary says their dates always involved a good-natured argument or two. When he came home from work, they would sit on the back patio, drinking gin and tonics, and delve deep into the problems of the world. They traveled the world together, having adventures. They raised two children in their forty-seven years together. "Not nearly long enough," Mary says. In 2007, Dave was diagnosed with amyotrophic lateral sclerosis—ALS or Lou Gehrig's disease.

Mary says at first they laughed when he couldn't do things; it was funny. But as his body slowly turned against him, as Mary became his caretaker, she began to grieve. People who have had parents or partners with Alzheimer's know this experience: the grief happens before they're dead, it's almost preemptive. A widower I know told me that when his wife died, he felt no sadness, because he'd grieved twenty years ago. Mary said in the three years that Dave's body slowly fell apart, her grief was about realizing what they had made together. She had so many things to say to him about their life and her love, and she struggled with what to say so he wouldn't feel bad for leaving her.

Dave died in 2010 very quickly; he'd been alert, asking questions, and then he wasn't. Mary calls it merciful. She says it was a relief, that the grief now comes in waves. She remembers meals he used to cook that she can't duplicate. She remembers those conversations on the patio with gin and tonics. She had to get a new car recently, and it was so hard to let go of the one she had, because Dave had bought it. It was just a stupid car, but it was his. It's hard now when she travels, because she sees couples hand in hand or not even touching but with that obvious "we're together" vibe. She teared up when she told me about that. "Who am I going to tell now?" she asked. She sees such beautiful things on her travels, and all she wants to do is tell Dave because he would love it. Would have.

Soon after he died, Mary was driving somewhere, and she said out loud, "I can't do this, God." And plain as day, she heard, "You will be taken care of." And she has been, maybe because of all the people she herself takes care of. As the children come into church, she greets all of them as if they're her friends, because they are. She helps her older friend down the aisle for Communion.

In the ALS support group she joined years ago, she sees other widows who have lost not only their husbands but also their social circles. Who wants a widow around, reminding everyone of the inevitability of death? Who wants her when she's only half of who she was, the other half ripped away? Widowers are no different and experience this same isolation. The death of a spouse, or even divorce, is bigger than the person, just as their marriage was bigger than the two of them.

I have a friend whose marriage ended badly. They were passionate people whose marriage was full of argument and emotion and deep love. As the marriage was ending, my friend told me through painful sobs that it felt as if their marriage had been a living thing. She said there was something bigger than each of them and bigger than the two combined, and that was their marriage, as though the space between them had substance, weight, energy. Their marriage had a life of its own. And it had died.

I've carried her pain with me over the years. I've had conversations with many people whose relationships have ended—friendships, romantic partnerships, parent-child relationships—and they have similar experiences. There was something there that was more than the two of them, something that feels like it died. And with that death came the feeling of being left behind. Of being alone. Of an empty spot at the table or in our experience of the world. Even though our rational minds know we aren't the only ones to feel this emptiness, it feels like we are. It feels like emptiness is all there is.

Maybe now you're expecting me to jump to some good news. I'll just say something like "But there's more beyond that emptiness; there's hope." There is, but maybe we jump to that too soon. We're uncomfortable with people's grief, so we want to find the right words to make them happier. But there aren't any right words. There is grief and there is hope, and they don't cancel each other out. Widows make us uncomfortable because they reveal our own closeness to death. The widows in scripture are actual widows with actual stories, but they're also metaphors for our own loneliness and loss. Maybe we need to sit with those feelings for a while before we try to get rid of them.

Our communal relationship as Christians is a living thing just as much as our romantic or platonic relationships. In Paul's words, we are all part of the body of Christ. I would go further and say the human family is part of the same body. Mary is as much a part of me as my leg or ear is. We are more than a community, we are necessary to one another. The body is not whole if we leave out even one widow or orphan or foreigner or whomever they stand in for in your life. We are corporate, not individual—or at any rate, not only individual. When the Hebrew writers speak of God's salvation, of the Promised Land, of God's pleasure or anger, it's almost always third person plural—"y'all." It's not that I do justice and love kindness, so I'm right with God. We as a community do justice and love kindness, and *we* are right with God. A preacher friend of mine said recently, "We don't love each other because it's a rule we have to follow and so we can get into the kingdom. When we love each other, that *is* the kingdom."

So it is the vulnerable people of the world who show us our humanity—widows, yes, and shell-shocked refugee children, survivors of a mass shooting in a gay club, the conservative minority in a liberal-majority college, people living on the streets by choice or by chance, children trafficked into sex work out of the foster system, and so many more. How we respond when we see them speaks volumes about our humanity and faith. We can learn more, we can ask what they need, we can advocate for justice, and we can sit and listen, as Mary does with the old people she spends time with.

The widows in the Bible remind us to care for anyone we meet who needs it. And they remind us that we are widows of a sort, and we need caring for, too.

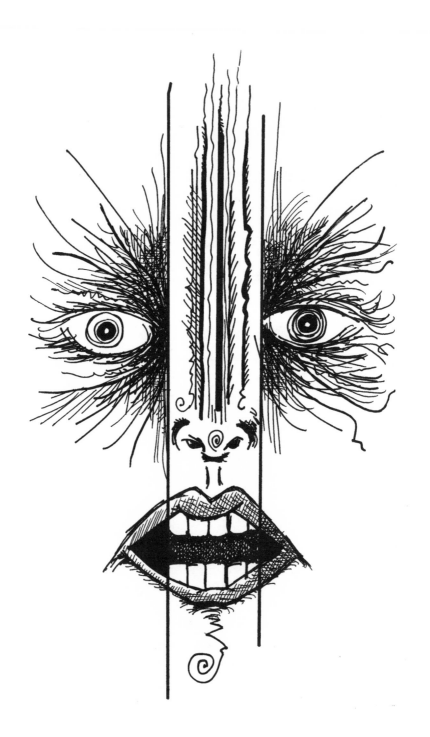

Jerusalem

I Don't Love You, and I Always Will

For thus says the Lord GOD: I will deliver you into the hands of those whom you hate, into the hands of those from whom you turned in disgust; and they shall deal with you in hatred, and take away all the fruit of your labor, and leave you naked and bare, and the nakedness of your whorings shall be exposed. Your lewdness and your whorings have brought this upon you, because you played the whore with the nations, and polluted yourself with their idols.

—EZEKIEL 23:28–30

To start with, the chapters from the prophet Ezekiel I'm about to share with you are really disturbing, and not at all in a funny way. I mean, I'll probably make some halfhearted jokes because this book isn't supposed to be a complete downer, and anyway, I can't help it—it's a defense mechanism. There's a lot to defend against in the book of Ezekiel. This is the chapter I most want to use the f-bomb in, but my editor tells me we can't. Which I get, I really do. There's a reason ancient rabbis had an age restriction of thirty-five years old to read Ezekiel. This is rough, folks, so if you have issues with an abusive spouse or parent or with the existence of rape (and why wouldn't you?), you might want to skip this chapter. Or maybe you want to get a stiff drink and power through, because maybe I can help us come out the other side in one piece.

The prophet Ezekiel was one foul-mouthed dude. His book is never translated accurately, because the translators take one look at the Hebrew and squeal like junior high boys seeing a tampon. "We can't translate *that*," they say in hushed tones, looking over their shoulders at all of Christianity. "They would freak out." Seriously, we would. I mentioned in the Song of Songs chapter that her book isn't translated accurately either, what with the midsections of ivory and whatnot. This is much, much worse. When Ezekiel goes on about Jerusalem's whoring of herself, that's a nice way to put it. This is one of the places where the f-bomb would be appropriate; just replace "whoring," and you'll get the drift.

Ezekiel was also a performance artist. He built a little model of the city of Jerusalem with all the streets and buildings and walls. Then he lay down on his side near it and didn't move for almost a year to symbolize God's judgment of Israel. While lying on his side, he prophesied against the model city. Can you see it, ranting about Jerusalem's sins while reclining near his little Lego model? He's famous for creating a special whole-grain bread to eat during his model-city siege, except the recipes you can get online fail to mention that God told him to bake it in a fire made with human excrement. He was grossed out by that one, so he convinced God to let him use cow pies instead. Later, he cut off all his hair as a sign of God's judgment, burning some, cutting some into the wind, and binding some into the hem of his clothing. All of these were meant to be dramatic visual aids to accompany his accusations that the people deserved their fate.

The fate he was bemoaning was the nation's exile to Babylon. Israel and Judah had once been a single country but had long since split. They'd both been invaded and occupied by various neighboring powers, the most recent being Assyria. When Babylon rose to power and took over, its army destroyed the temple in Jerusalem where God lived (the innermost part of the temple was where the hem of God's robe swirled about majestically, and where God's footstool, the Ark of the Covenant, sat waiting for God to relax). If Babylon could destroy God's house, where was God? Then Babylon took all the important people back to its capital. Political, religious, and economic leaders, the upper class, even the middle classes—all were made into refugees. Ezekiel was one of the first to be deported to Babylon, and as the people began pouring in, he tried to help them make sense of what had happened. His way of making sense was not comforting at all.

I'm going to tell you a couple of infamous stories where the prophet used the metaphor of marriage for the relationship between God and the Jewish people. We've seen this before with bridal mysticism in the Song of Songs. Ezekiel was much, much less happy about the relationship.

In the first story, God was strolling down the road and saw Baby Jerusalem lying in the grass on the shoulder. It's a metaphor; cities were often spoken about with female pronouns, as boats are. Looking closer, God saw that the baby was a newborn, still covered in blood and mucus from the birth, but dried and crusty. God looked around and saw no one nearby, no one to love her, no one who'd left her there. She'd been abandoned to die of exposure. God decided she should live, and it was so. The baby Jerusalem grew up and hit sexual maturity. God fell in love with her, cleaned her up, married her, and made sweet, sweet love to her. God gave her all the things—jewelry, fancy clothing, perfumes, flowers for her hair—and said, "Look what I do for you, baby."

But this sexy, grown-up Jerusalem was enamored of her own beauty and took lovers in the form of all the other nations around. "Oh, Egypt, you're so handsome and strong. Oh, Assyria, you're so big. Oh, Chaldea, I can't wait to be with you," she said. The text speaks extensively of her "whorings," like, a lot. She was insatiable, and the text is insatiable in talking about it. She wasn't just unfaithful to God, her husband who had so graciously saved her, she also melted down her jewelry and made "idols" of her lovers to "whore herself" with. Dildos. It's talking about dildos. Then she had her children murdered, which was apparently what her lovers' gods wanted. And then she did all of that whoring and idolatry in public with random passers-by. Finally, it turns out she wasn't a common prostitute who was paid for her labors, which might have made it just a tad more respectable. No—plot twist—she paid all of those lovers to sleep with her. She was, according to God, a special kind of whore.

But wait, there's more. God said, "Therefore, O whore, hear the word of the Lord." God got all her lovers together and "uncovered her nakedness" in front of them. That can mean several things, from revoking the covenant they have together to actually having sex with her in front of them. Presumably against her will. The crowd beat her with stones and cut her with swords, and God egged them all on. Then and only then did God's anger dissipate. There's a little denouement where God said, "Look, I'm sorry I had to be like that, but you totally deserved it, bitch. No one was as nasty as you, not even your whore sisters like Sodom. You *should* be ashamed. But, you know, I'm going to give you everything back, because I'm a kind and generous husband." So, at least there's that.

The second story is about two sisters who are stand-ins for Samaria and Jerusalem. While they were still unmarried, they were whores, letting the other nations caress their breasts and such. God married them both, knowing what they were into, and was then surprised that they continued their sexual adventures. Wife Samaria didn't give up her previous lovers from Egypt and took on more from Assyria. Like Jerusalem in the first story, she made "idols" of her lovers to use in her own bedroom. God was pissed and turned her over to the lovers, who "uncovered her nakedness" and killed her. Totally fair, right?

Wife Jerusalem saw all this and was undeterred. Her "lustings and whorings" were even more intense, and she had sex with all the men from all the countries. Jerusalem's lovers, the text says, were hung like donkeys, and their ejaculations were like that of horses. Yow. Then Ezekiel goes on at length about the retribution God made Jerusalem's lovers take out on her: killing her, burning her survivors, cutting off her nose and ears, stripping her, beating her, possibly raping her, not necessarily in that order. Seriously, it's alarming how much effort Ezekiel puts into this bit of violence. And Jerusalem will punish herself even—she will drink from the cup of horror and desolation that was her sister's and chew on its broken shards and tear out her own breasts because God is so angry. And then, breaking the fourth wall, Ezekiel says, "Let this be a lesson to all women not to whore around." Not just Jerusalem as a personified city, but all women, watch yourselves.

Do you need a minute to absorb all that? Maybe go take a brisk walk and wash your face? I can wait.

I am straight up furious about these two chapters. Why the hell is this in the Bible? Let me be honest with you for a moment: I didn't know this shit was in there until I went to seminary. I was twenty-six years old. Portraying God who created us and loves us and wants the best for us as an abusive lover is counterproductive and viscerally damaging. What does this say not only to people who have been abused but also to the rest of us? God is slow to anger, except when he's not. God is so angry with you for whatever it is you've done that he will make your life miserable and then let someone murder you. Or everything bad that happens to you is punishment from God ("you" being an individual or an entire nation, take your pick). I can't believe that. I just can't.

Too many women in the history of humanity have been abused by husbands or lovers in exactly this way. The woman may or may not have done something wrong, the husband gets angry and hurts her, and then his anger is sated and he apologizes, saying he'll never do it again. "I'm so sorry, baby. Why you gotta make me so angry?" And then it starts all over; it's a cycle. I know, in Ezekiel's time, they probably didn't hear these oracles in light of cycles of abuse; that's fairly recent. A number of modern commentators implore the reader not to impose our understandings of love and abuse on ancient texts. Fair enough. But abusive spouses have been around since the beginning.

And we are *supposed* to be revolted: Ezekiel is performing for us, trying to make us see how hurtful our behavior is. We are almost blind to it. We bemoan how numb we've become to violence, how we can't be shocked anymore, and it's true. Disasters happen, we are rightfully sad, we send off a check, and nothing changes. After a while, we end up with outrage fatigue; things are shitty out there, but we don't have the energy for outrage any more. If the shooting at Sandy Hook Elementary School didn't shake us up into doing something different, nothing will. But then we turn around and say the most hateful things to each other online, insulting each other for political views, insisting on all-or-nothing solutions, leaking personal images, even threatening each other with death. We don't see our own violence. We don't see how our normal, selfish actions, online or not, feed the violence of the world. To paraphrase the cartoon Pogo, we've seen the enemy, but we can't see that he is us.

But that's not new. Our great-great-grandparents in Jerusalem in 586 BCE were numb to it, too. And also selfish and rude. So all the prophets use extreme, insulting, offensive language to shock the people into feeling again. "Wake up to what you're doing!" they say, while punching us in the collective gut. "Wake the F up!"

What we're doing is idolatry, putting something or someone in the place of God. For Ezekiel, that was the political and military alliances Jerusalem had formed with neighboring nations. They were supposed to be allied with God and God alone. They were supposed to care for orphans and widows. They were supposed to remember the Sabbath day and keep it holy. But they didn't. And we don't. Therefore, every bad thing that could possibly happen to them as a nation and as individuals was because God was angry and heartbroken. When they (and we) choose not-God, they (and we) leave ourselves open to retribution.

I am still pissed off that these stories exist at all, whether in scripture or in our lives. But I also understand them, even if it makes me feel incredibly uncomfortable to say so. If I'm honest, I want a God who gets angry—not irrationally angry, not abusive or vengeful, but still angry at suffering and injustice. I don't want a soft, fluffy God seeing the pain here and feeling nothing. I want widows and orphans and people being abused to be seen and heard and to find new life. I want a God who is angry at spiritual rhetoric that paints women as sluts and less than men. I want a God who is angry at the denial of the black experience of violence *and* who is angry at the deaths of police officers. I think that's exactly what we have. God is angry and Ezekiel wants us to be as well.

And God is heartbroken. The thing is, God gave us free will. God wants to be chosen, not followed by automatons because we can't do anything else, so in the garden called Eden, God gave us a choice. And because we can and do choose not-God, God is heartbroken. *That* I can believe—God watching us and thinking, "I love you, I made you. Why do you keep choosing someone else?" This is at the core of our human story: separation from God. We think God can't possibly love us, can't possibly exist even, so we'll have to make love and connection and real justice happen ourselves. We see what the prophets saw: that there is no one to stand in the breach between love and nothingness, that bad things happen to good people and to bad people and to all of us who are both. We feel separate from the experience of God, so we try to recreate it by ourselves. Separation from God can become functional atheism, which seems to me like a natural response to the world. Within the church, we've chosen to name our response to feeling separate "sin."

Why should we remember these two stories about Wife Jerusalem and not just ignore them? Because they're calls to action. Whether you want to ignore the violent sexual metaphor and delve straight into the social justice Ezekiel is rooting for, or whether it's the metaphor itself you react against, what's it calling you to do?

Does it wake you up to the ways you hurt yourself and others? Does it call you to take up arms against toxic masculinity? Does it ask you to choose kindness so these stories can be forgotten in a cloud of caring witnesses?

I chose to write about Jerusalem because it is so painful. God's heart is broken by our actions, and our hearts are broken by how Ezekiel talks about it. It's not simplistic; it's a reminder that there's no easy answer to our questions. These chapters look like the opposite of how we understand God. They're also exactly what a lot of the world thinks our God is like, because *we* are like that. We shame women for their sexual desire; we abandon each other in time of need; we choose a presidential candidate or job security over God; we attack and destroy. Our history as Christians and Jews is not all good. We are kind of a mess, and the stories we tell reflect that. They're hurtful and confounding, and we need them so we can be honest about who we are. Sometimes we are angry for justice, and sometimes we are angry for violent, bloody vengeance. It's not pretty, but it's true.

Disturbing passages of scripture aren't less disturbing if we ignore them. The evil of this world isn't wiped out by good; it lives alongside it. Death isn't destroyed by life; they walk hand in hand. But the experience of good, love, light, and life can transform evil, hate, darkness, and life. Let us choose the complex, the beautiful, the kind, the transformative, and as Ezekiel also says, "turn, then, and live."

Susanna's Choice

> Then Susanna cried out with a loud voice, and said, "O
> eternal God, you know what is secret and are aware of all
> things before they come to be; you know that these men
> have given false evidence against me. And now I am to
> die, though I have done none of the wicked things that they
> have charged against me!"
> The Lord heard her cry.
>
> —SUSANNA 42–44

I used to lead a Bible study for twentysomething professionals. A couple of them worked for our local multinational corporation that rhymes with Flocter & Flamble, one was considering seminary, a couple others were teachers, and one was a librarian. They were wicked smart and engaged, asked challenging questions, and were some of the most loving people I've known. A lot of our discussions revolved around how to find ourselves in the stories, how to identify with the characters. Gotta make it relevant, you know? To my great surprise, these smart, engaged, loving people often simply couldn't do it. They'd say, "It's an interesting story, but what am I supposed to *do* with it?" After particularly difficult passages, my friend Jill became famous for saying, "I feel poorly about that."

Now, I hope it doesn't sound like I'm mocking my friends, especially since they have become soul-friends over the years. They had the same problem with scripture that lots of people have: it feels two-dimensional. How do we get past cultural assumptions and hundreds of years of history to the people it's about and for? How do we do that now with people in the same room with us? How do we look past the specifics of people's lives to our similarities? For the moment, let's go with the two-dimensional thing as an entry point into one story: Susanna.

Imagine a cartoon character. Any one will do: early Mickey Mouse or Sleeping Beauty or even a Roy Lichtenstein painting. Imagine what the character is wearing, the color of the character's skin, maybe how the character looks when he, she, or it is singing a jaunty tune. Notice how the character is drawn (a thick black line around the outside or more softly colored? huge eyes, flat color, maybe even that dotted coloring they used to do in the newspapers?). Consider how the character interacts with the world around: characters throw vases or put on coats or fight monsters, they fall in love, they throw tantrums, they make breakfast burritos. But also, they're completely flat. They're two dimensions on a flat plane, moving only because our brains trick us into thinking so. This is, in a silly way maybe, how we sometimes look at scripture.

Now take that same kind of image you've built in your head, that same style of drawing, and imagine a young woman. This is Susanna. She's beautiful in that flat, cartoony way. Her clothes are simple and modest. She's of Middle Eastern descent with dark hair, olive skin, full lips, and wide, almond-shaped eyes, and her head is covered reverentially. She's in a walled garden full of trees and flowers and twittering birds; maybe she's a bit like Cinderella, singing to them as she wanders the garden. Maybe it's a vegetable garden, and she looks more like Rosie the Riveter. Her clothing is simple overalls, something she can wear to get on her knees in the dirt and get to work. Maybe she's got on her green plastic gardening clogs and a wide-brimmed hat. She carries a basket for the harvest. Or some tools to fix the loose armrest on the bench. Or a book to contemplate under the clove tree. And on one end of the garden is a lovely pond, clear blue, surrounded by choice water plants—lilies and cattails—buzzing with dragonflies.

This is her garden. Hers and her husband's. Susanna is married to Joakim, Man of God. Together, they're kind of the local power couple, beautiful and upright and rich and good. It's all straight-forward, the way we think about cartoons—simple, pretty, fun. They live here in a beautiful house with a beautiful garden under the beautiful sky, and the beautiful people come to visit, and it's all just simply beautiful.

Only it's not that simple. Susanna walks in her garden, unaware of the bad guys lurking behind the trees. In our two-dimensional world, the bad guys have long, curled mustaches or are hunchbacks or wear black hats. Or maybe they're fine to look at but have a light in their eyes that unsettles you. They sneak around like villains in old melodramas and watch Susanna from the shadows and lust after her. These bad guys, surprisingly, are elders and judges in the Jewish community, upright and blameless. They meet every day at Susanna and Joakim's house to settle disputes and share God's wisdom. These men know their duties to justice and compassion, and—the story goes—they set those duties aside and willfully turn their eyes to a married woman. They want her and are embarrassed by their want. The way the narrator presents them, they are creepy but still easily dismissed because their evil is so obvious.

One afternoon, after the elders have fulfilled their duties to judge the disputes of the people inside Susanna and Joakim's house, they say to one another, "Great to see you today. Good work on the Josephson case. Hey, listen, I've gotta run. Lunch meeting with the scribes; you know how they are. Yeah, catch you tomorrow." And they head in different directions. Then each circles back, maybe taking a comically circuitous route. Each returns to the garden gate, where they all look at each other in shock—shock, I tell you! Their embarrassment at being caught quickly turns to conniving smirks. "Are you thinking what I'm thinking?" They check their calendars and arrange to meet again the following day to watch together (nothing goes better with illicit sexual desire than a creepy buddy to share it with, you know). Knowing the Jewish law as they do, they hatch a totally legal and not at all questionable plan, twirling their mustaches all the while.

The following day is hot—one of those days when you can see the air shimmer over the land and your skin prickles because you've run out of sweat. Susanna finishes weeding or reading or praying, and she looks across the garden to the lovely, clear, blue pond. Just looking at its flat blue surface makes her long for a swim. How refreshing it would be—maybe with a little olive oil soap to moisturize, a loofa to smooth her heels. She calls her servants and asks that they bring out some things—maybe a nice, soft towel. "Calgon, take me away," she thinks. On the way to do her bidding, the servants lock the garden gate, not noticing even for a moment the two elders, hidden behind trees, watching, waiting.

Before Susanna has even undone a single button, they leap out from behind the trees and run toward her, twin looks of glee and lust on their faces. "Hey, gorgeous," they call. "We're all alone here in the garden. You want to come have sex with us, don't you? We're nice guys, you know; we deserve it. And if you don't, we'll tell everyone you have a lover and that's why you're alone here in the garden." Ooh, entitlement and threats—what a pickup line.

And this is where the story shifts abruptly from a two-dimensional kind of malice, a simple, almost mischievous story, to the grimy real world. Instead of *Toy Story*, now we're watching *CSI: Israel*. The clear outlines blur. Suddenly, we can smell sweat and pollen and fear. Suddenly, it's uncomfortably familiar to women who have been catcalled or groped or threatened. Suddenly, it's a documentary of women pushed into prostitution or raped and then blamed for the horrors that happened to them. Though there's eventually a happy ending filled with silly word-plays, the story isn't beautiful anymore.

Susanna looks between the two of them with increasing panic. She has backed up against a tree and now feels the sinking in her gut as she realizes that she cannot get away, not with the tree at her back and their grasping hands at her front. The prickle in her skin that came from the heat is now from revulsion and the scratch of the tree bark. She thinks of the servants and her own beloved husband in the house only steps away. They might as well be miles away. She remembers stories whispered about and lamented over of someone's daughter or cousin or friend taken in rape and how she could never be married because of the shame. She remembers their children—never really part of their families, always just a little outside. She remembers how those women had a quiet desperation behind their eyes. She is angry that these trusted counselors would betray her and her husband and even the Jewish people. She's angry that she has little choice. Yet she does still have a choice.

Susanna is not only beautiful, she is intelligent. She knows the law. She knows she has a choice, terrible though it is: adultery or death. Susanna knows that her word as a woman and as a person alone in the garden will not be believed. She knows that the two men in front of her will serve as each other's alibi. She knows she cannot consent to their demands. And so she chooses a third option.

Susanna cries aloud, a soul-deep, bowel-deep cry of frustration and pain, like the cry of the people Israel in slavery and in exile when God heard and answered. The only answer now is her servants running into the garden, seeing her compromised and making assumptions. "How could she?" they think. "What a hussy," they think. "Asking for it, I bet. Look at that outfit," they think. And they are ashamed of her.

The following day, Susanna is put on trial for her licentiousness. It's hot, hotter even than the day before, but Susanna cannot think of her lovely, clear, blue pond but only of the desperate and quite possibly short future before her. Like women the world over who have been burned with acid or strangled by jealous husbands or accused of witchcraft or any manner of sins they did not commit, Susanna kneels and prays and weeps. And the elders, those upright and wise judges, in the sight of the people come to see Susanna's fall, in the sight of her parents, her husband, her relatives, and her children, they order that her veil be removed. Actually, the word is more visceral than that, more brutal—not *removed* but *stripped*. She is stripped naked in front of everyone she knew. Perhaps those lechers, not having gotten what they wanted in private, determined to ogle her in public.

Either way, they begin to pontificate about how they had found her in the embrace of her lover, wantonly spreading her legs where anyone, really, could peek over the garden wall—or hide behind a tree maybe—and see all her secrets. She probably wanted to be caught, to be seen, just as they are all seeing her now. So filthy, showing off her naked body here in the town square. They claim to have torn open the gates to accuse the two of them but could not catch the lover, as he was too strong for those who spend their time prayerfully studying God's word. They warm to their subject, expounding upon how Israel needs to be kept pure as God's bride and how Susanna needs to be an example to all of them of the punishment God will render when they are found wanting.

They put their hands on her head while they speak, and Susanna shudders with revulsion that they would touch her.

The people, thinking the elders to be honest, trustworthy men, believe them.

They sentence Susanna to death.

Again she cries out as Israel has cried out for reprieve.

And this time God answers.

God nudges a young man named Daniel (yes, that Daniel, but pre–lion's den and furnace of fire), who calls out, "No! This trial is a mockery. You haven't got all the evidence. Justice doesn't mean believing the first accusation. Seriously, haven't you ever read a murder mystery?"

The people agree that this is a fair point, and they settle in to hear what Daniel will say.

The story gets a little silly again at this point, which is odd.

Daniel says, "Take these men to opposite sides of the town square, and I will interview them separately." And thus Daniel invents the police procedural drama.

To the first man, he says, "You filthy viper, unworthy to even clean up after my pet pig, tell me the truth: Under what tree did you see Susanna and her lover?"

He says, "Under the clove tree."

And Daniel says, "Your words condemn you. God will cleave you in two because of your lies."

Do you see what he did there? "Clove tree" and "cleave you"? It's there in the Greek, too.

And thus Daniel invents witty banter.

To the second man, he says, "You whoremonger, you monster, you sexual predator, tell me the truth: Under which tree did you see Susanna and her lover?"

And he says, "Under the yew tree."

And Daniel said, "Your words condemn you. God will hew you in two because of your lies."

See what he did there? "Yew tree" and "hew you"?

And thus Daniel invents the bad cop–bad cop routine.

Oh, and he also proves Susanna's innocence.

Speaking of whom, where is she during this bit? The bad guys get put to death for impugning an innocent woman, Susanna's family and neighbors rejoice, God is praised, and Daniel develops a reputation as a wise detective.

And Susanna, she's blameless the entire time. She did nothing wrong—what, like being a beautiful woman who says no to a creepy come-on? That's called self-possession. She is not silent like Dinah and Bathsheba and Jephtha's daughter before her. She has a voice and uses it to cry out to God about the injustice of the world, as did Hagar and Rebekah before her. That's called prophecy. She calls attention to the threat from within the Jewish community: the people who are supposed to care for the vulnerable but who exploit them instead. These are the people whose power makes them untouchable and frightening to confront. Susanna calls them out, and Daniel picks up what she is laying down.

Here at the end, it becomes his story, not hers. Daniel is the champion of the faith that God brings in to beat back the enemy. He's the hero who saves the damsel and brings enlightenment to the people. That's all true, of course, but Susanna's heroism is lost in the accolades for Daniel. She is a good lawyer; she refuses to participate in the elders' evil. Who is the hero here? Whose story is it?

That question is probably a red herring. It's not as though Daniel comes riding in triumphantly to take control of the narrative from an untrustworthy, sexually suspect woman. He's just living his life, doing his thing. Susanna isn't just a victim; she sees clearly that she needs help and demands it. It's Susanna's story, and it's Daniel's story.

The story also belongs to us, to those of us reading it now. I mean, you're not a wealthy Jewish woman in the second century BCE faced with a choice between public and private shame. Probably not. But you have been faced with difficult choices, someone has overshadowed your story at one time or another, and you have been the one people scorned, whether you deserved it or not. Susanna's story isn't two-dimensional, it's layered and complex, and so is yours. All of our stories change depending on who is telling them and what that person wants. One person says Susanna couldn't possibly speak for herself convincingly, and another says she only needed someone to believe her. Even my retelling of Susanna's story has an agenda: she is her own hero, she is as fierce as any woman, and male privilege is still an issue today.

How many times growing up did I complain that some boy was snapping my bra strap or saying sexual things to me that I didn't really understand but knew in my bones were creepy and threatening? How many times was I told, "He's just doing it because he likes you," as though that made it completely fine? How many times have men in authority taken it upon themselves to give me tutorials on tasks that I already knew well how to do? I'm no wilting flower; I'm more of a steamroller, doing my own thing anyway. Outwardly, I slapped them, I ignored them, I sneered, and I spoke incredulously, hoping they would stop. Inwardly, I felt alone, abandoned, as if my story weren't as important. So I made it important. I will be listened to, by God, not dismissed.

When we start to remove the layers of our own stories, we are laid bare as Susanna was in the town square. Maybe we should use a more brutal word like *stripped*, because being vulnerable and letting other people see who we are and what has happened in our lives is unpleasant. When we cry out for help, we are showing our own nakedness, and that is as heroic as the people coming to our aid.

3

Christian Women

Early on in my pastoral career, the political problem was how I looked. One of my first supervisors asked me to dress with more professionalism than nice sweaters and jeans, so I arrived one day in a neat brown-and-white pinstripe blazer and vest with light-purple checked palazzo pants. I felt like I'd nailed it—slick but with some sass. He took one look and asked if I'd intended to look like a clown. Later on, I did wild things to my hair—shaved it for a while; dyed it purple, blue, or pink; had frosted tips—but I was a youth pastor, so no big deal. Except I was also preaching every few weeks to not-the-youth. They couldn't take me seriously.

When the pastor is a woman, questioning how she looks and what that communicates becomes normal conversation, more so than with male pastors. We can't be too sexy (which can mean anything, really), and we can't be too dowdy. Many of the first female pastors in the late twentieth century styled themselves in a very masculine fashion so they would be acceptable to congregations used to seeing men up front. Very similar things were happening in the business world. Even more, just the fact that we are women means that our looks are more scrutinized. Do I look tired? Is my nail polish chipped? "You look so dressed up today" can sometimes be code for "dat ass." My Chuck Taylors matched to the liturgical color of the season are cause for comment most Sundays in every church where I preach. I could stop wearing them, but I like them. They're part of how I see myself—indie church nerd. I once got taken aside and asked earnestly why I thought it was okay that my two-year-old son quietly sat next to me on the floor while I preached that evening.

How women look when we're up front, taking on leadership or voicing opinions, is still odd to our culture. Much of the criticism of Hillary Clinton is masked misogyny. There's a conversation to be had about her record, but our culture as a whole doesn't know what to do with women in leadership. It doesn't need to be this way. Women in the early church were disciples, deacons, theologians, mystics, politicians. Our mothers and grandmothers and great-grandmothers were in that great line of disciples and mystics, too. We've forgotten their stories or changed them, but they're still there, waiting for us to read them and be changed by them.

At the Well and on the Road

Women Back-Talking God

> Then the woman left her water-jar and went back to the city. She said to the people, "Come and see a man who told me everything I have ever done! He cannot be the Messiah, can he?"
>
> —JOHN 4:28–29

I don't know if you're aware of this, but back-talking God is a long-standing tradition. Cain, the first murderer, did it when God asked after his brother's health: "Whatever, God, I'm not in charge of Abel, am I?" The prophets as a whole say, "Really, me? What are you on about?" when God comes calling. The entire book of Job is about pushing back and saying, "What are you thinking, God? How does any of this make sense?" Mary pushes Jesus to do something about the lamentable lack of wine at the wedding at Cana and then ignores his response when he doesn't want to. These folks seemed to get that God can take it when we ask questions, when we're defensive, and even when we directly contradict. (My dad used to say to me, "You're so contrary." To which I'd respond, "No, I'm not!")

Okay, so maybe it's not exactly back-talking; it's more arguing. But it's significant, because so many of us grew up thinking that we couldn't question God, we couldn't ask why to our church, we couldn't have doubt about anything we were told. It's a false dichotomy between faith and doubt: these back-talkers aren't filthy doubters because they didn't have faith in God, and they're not puppets, taking God at God's word with no question. They question *because* they have faith—or even because they *want* faith. It's important to admit our not knowing what the hell is going on when we're talking about Jesus. God's not some wilting flower; we push back because we care about the relationship enough to understand it and make it better.

Cases in point: the Samaritan woman at the well and the Canaanite woman on the road.

At the well, Jesus stopped for a long, cool glass of water. It was hot, he'd been walking all over Samaria and Israel, and he was tired. So he sat. The woman came to draw water. And that, as they say, was where it all began. The longest theological discussion in the Gospels is between Jesus and this woman. He was the wandering prophet, wild-haired, sweaty, with the gleam of adventure and wisdom in his eyes. She was the outcast and sometime theologian, proud, put together, and with the sheen of intelligence and sadness in her eyes.

He said to her, as men had said to women for centuries, "Give me a drink," and he meant both "I'm thirsty" and "I know the old stories of Jacob and Moses at the well, and I know that question means marriage sometimes, but I don't really mean that. Mostly." And he meant, "I know you have questions. Quench my thirst, and I'll quench yours."

She said to him, "You know you're not supposed to talk to me, right? I'm a woman for one thing, and I'm from your enemy Samaria, and also people think I'm kind of a slut, or they will after your friend John writes this story down, so you're just asking for trouble talking to me."

Jesus said to her, "Don't you know who I am?" John, who wrote the story down later, thought, "Get it? I AM?" It's kind of an in joke, because the Hebrew name for God is Yahweh, usually trans-lated "I Aм." Anyway, Jesus said to her, "I'm more than what I look like—as are you. See, I've got this living water. Want to know what that's about?"

She said to him, noticing that he didn't seem to care much about who she was, and with a teasing lilt to her voice, "You know, you're the one who asked me for water, since you don't have a bucket, so how the heck will you give me water? Got a secret up your sleeve? Think you're better than our com-mon great-grandfather Jacob, who built this well in the first place?" Maybe she cocked her fist on her hip and looked at him challengingly.

Jesus said to her, "Ah, you know exactly what I'm saying, don't you? The water in this well is tasty, yes, but you'll be thirsty again after drinking it, won't you? This water I'm talking about will become a river inside you—you know, metaphorically—and you will never be thirsty again. Ever."

She said to Jesus, knowing he was offering more than literal water, knowing this was a kind of verbal puzzle, and knowing her part in the matrimonial story of conversations at wells, "Oh God, yes."

Jesus smiled conspiratorially at her and said, "Would you go get your husband and bring him back here?"

She said to him, "You know I've got no husband."

He said to her, "Truth—you've had five, and the one you've got now isn't yours."

She said to him, "Damn, son, you're like Sherlock." (I know you want to know about the husbands. Don't worry, we'll come back to that.) With no segue whatsoever, she asked him her most pressing theological question. "You can see the truth of things, so answer me this, 'cause I've been thinking about it for a while: My people, the Samaritans, worship here at Mount Gerizim, where our common great-grandfathers worshipped, but I hear your people the Jews saying Jerusalem is the place. Which one is right? Because it seems like our cultures are at odds, and I do want to be faithful to Yahweh."

Jesus said to her, completely dropping the issue of her husband, "Soon the location won't matter, because we will all be worshipping God for real, face-to-face, not through a glass darkly, if you will. Because God is doing something for the world through the Jews, soon you'll feel God's presence in a whole new world, a new fantastic point of view—"

The woman rolled her eyes and interrupted, "Yes, this makes so much sense. I know that the one that God has chosen and set apart—y'all call him the Messiah—is on the way. Not sure exactly what he'll do, but I've a few suggestions for him. When's he getting here?"

He said to her, grinning, "It's me, friend. I am he."

She grinned back at him, triumphant and thrilled and overwhelmed at what he'd told her. They stared at each other in silence, delighted, the space between them seeming to have weight, substance, life.

Then the disciples returned from their errands in town. When they saw her, they, too, stared in silence, but it was the awkward kind where you don't know what to say but you feel like you ought to say something. They stayed away because they didn't want the trouble of talking to her, seeing as they could her obvious outsiderness. Where she was self-possessed and articulate, they were afraid and unaware of themselves. She looked at them. She looked back at Jesus and his delighted smile. She left her water jugs and her spiritual baggage there and walked back to the city, head held high. She knocked on people's doors and tapped them on the shoulder in the market. She said, "You would not believe what just happened to me. I met the Messiah, I think. He's a little slippery, but he's so great. He told me about everything I've ever done. You should go see him, too."

And a miracle happened: they listened to her. The conversation opened her eyes, not to her shame but to God's presence and promise.

I get pretty frustrated reading commentaries about this story. Almost all of them make a big deal—like, pages and pages of discussion—about her sexual proclivities. There are theologies where each of those husbands are allegories for political allies Samaria has, which is bad because God is supposed to be the husband and you're a big hussy if you ally with anyone else. There are theologies where she's clearly a woman of ill repute, and that adds to the commenters' condescension to her: she's even more of an outsider and couldn't *really* understand what Jesus was saying anyway. The poor dear, let's explain it all to her in small words. It's interesting that commenters seem to care more about these five or six husbands than Jesus does. As is the case for Mary Magdalene, who was probably not a prostitute but a moneyed patroness for Jesus, if the woman at the well is a big hussy, it's a beautiful story of redemption and acceptance that she hears Jesus. But if she's not, it's a beautiful story of a strong woman affecting the spread of the good news. See, awkward.

It would seem that the woman at the well was one of the few people who picked up what Jesus was laying down.

The Canaanite woman on the road did, too. Her story is told twice in the Gospels, which is peculiar because Jesus doesn't come off very well either time. It reminds me of what my husband says about Peter: he was the first bishop of Rome, a venerated figure in the early church, and we have dozens of stories in scripture about his being a dolt. What wonderful humility he had to allow those stories to stand. Anyway, though this story is much shorter than that of the woman at the well, it is just as meaty.

Jesus was on the road again, moving from place to place, meeting people while out and about. Somewhere along the road, another outsider woman, this one from Canaan (we spit on them, *ptooi*), asked him to heal her daughter. As with others who asked for healing from Jesus, we don't know why she asked him in particular. There were all kinds of miracle workers around at the time; you couldn't spit on a Canaanite without hitting a miracle worker. Did she think, "Might as well; it could work"? Or did she think, "This guy, there's something about him that's beyond what I've seen, beyond what I understand. He's . . . the one we've been waiting for, son of David, wonderful counselor, mighty god, everlasting father, prince of peace"? Maybe she broke out in song as well.

Jesus at first didn't respond to her at all, and when he did, it was insulting. First he said he didn't come for the outsiders but for the insiders, the Jews. Then he said, "It's not fair to take the children's food and throw it to the dogs." In case the insult isn't obvious, the children are the Jews, and the dogs—filthy, bug-ridden, less-than-human dogs—are the Canaanites. Rude.

But she was desperate for her daughter's life and not as dumb as people thought. She took Jesus' insult and both owned it ("Sure, call me a dog; they're still part of the family. Sticks and stones, brother") and turned it back around ("Dogs eat the stuff that falls on the floor. I'll take whatever's left over, because your very special children in Israel aren't eating it, are they?"). Need some ice for that burn, Jesus?

It's not clear in the text what Jesus' motivation was in this exchange. In the end, he said something like "Well done, friend, your faith is strong, particularly in the face of insults from the Son of God. That's me; you got that, right? Your daughter is healed."

Commentators, trying to make sense of Jesus' response, suggest various things, all of which are unsatisfying. In the most popular, they say Jesus was testing the woman's faith. That seems kind of like a jerk move, considering they're talking about her daughter, a suffering human being. I think as well of how many other people he healed with no question—other foreigners, even oppressors and from a distance. But this woman, he had to see if she was really serious. This interpretation leads directly into the idea of faith healing—that if you're strong enough in your faith, God will heal you of whatever ails you. Rather than being a free gift from a loving God, healing has a price.

Perhaps he was questioning what she actually needed? When folks come to the door of the campus ministry where I work, asking for bus fare or a ride to an ATM, I know they need *something*. But it's usually not what they're asking for, or not *only* what they're asking for. Each person is different. Some need affordable housing. Some need sobriety. Some need a person to take them seriously. Was Jesus asking this woman, "What else do you need?"

It sure looks like he's genuinely uninterested in helping this woman because she's a foreigner. The way he talks to her sounds like he's parroting the rules of first-century Judaism. In such an emotionally painful situation, why would he do that? To be funny? Again, it seems unlikely, considering his frequent sparring with the Pharisees. There's something else going on here.

Did he, maybe—gasp—learn something from this Canaanite woman? I remember suggesting as much in some seminary class or other: maybe Jesus, being fully human in addition to being fully God, learned something about his message of love and how it was to be shared. Immediately, my classmates jumped to defend Jesus' omniscience. *Of course he didn't learn; he already knew all the things. Of course he didn't change; God doesn't change.* Never mind the number of times God changes God's mind in scripture. Never mind that Genesis tells us God repented of creating humans.

What happened to the woman after this story? It's a one-off. We don't know if she joined a synagogue or an early house church or if she followed behind Jesus as Mary Magdalene and Joanna did. We don't know if she thought Jesus was just a medical vending machine. We don't know if this was one of many experiences of God that would build up in her life, showing her a new reality.

The miracles for these two women are about more than healing, they're about overcoming prejudice and boundaries.

Like Ruth and Tamar, they're outsiders who understand what God's up to better than the insiders. What is that boundary for, anyway? Why put a line in the sand that keeps them out? We humans have been doing it for tens of thousands of years; it's hard to turn the ship around. We can't conceive of someone who thinks and does things differently having truth. We can't conceive of these women understanding more than the disciples. If they did, then we would have to think of them as better than the disciples, whatever that implies. But that's a false dichotomy. They're not better, just part of the same family. We can't conceive of Jesus' own compassion expanding when he interacts with someone new. He must have changed, but God can't change, so he must not be God. That's also a false dichotomy. God bless 'em, the disciples followed eagerly after Jesus, listened to the new things he was saying, and couldn't wrap their minds around it. These women don't have anything to prove. Because they are on the outside looking in, they can see the things the rest of us take for granted. They can ask the awkward questions that we've never thought of.

The woman at the well and the woman on the road show us we can argue with God—and with people who stand in the place of God. They're not unassailable; they can take it. I think a lot of us in the church don't believe that, though. Sometimes we have this driving need to protect God from challenge and doubt. We feel like we have to buttress the church to keep it standing against outside attacks. On campus, I run into a lot of students who have been hurt by the church or who have stood on the outside and wondered what the hell was going on inside. When we talk about it, sometimes they speak their hurt or their anger with pride, daring me to push back and convince them otherwise. Probably they've run into Christians who do that. My response is usually, "Absolutely the church has messed up. Is messed up. I understand your pain. I'm so sorry we've been so awful." Because the church and God can take our anger. Whether we're inside or outside the church, God listens to us and loves us for our faith and our questions alike.

At the well, Jesus intentionally broke social convention; on the road, he was challenged to do so. These women understood. We are all God's people. No one is a stranger to the family.

Mary and Martha

Jesus' Family of Choice

> When Mary came where Jesus was and saw him, she knelt
> at his feet and said to him, "Lord, if you had been here, my
> brother would not have died." When Jesus saw her weep-
> ing, and the Jews who came with her also weeping, he
> was greatly disturbed in spirit and deeply moved.
>
> —JOHN 11:32–33

One Sunday in 2016, just before I went in to lead the 11:00
a.m. service, my husband pulled me aside and said, "I'm so
sorry. There's been a bad shooting at a gay club in Orlando." I read
as many news stories as I could in a few minutes—one shooter,
forty dead, hostages, family waiting for identification—and sent a
message to my friends Nigel and JC, who own the biggest gay bar
in the city. Their bar Below Zero is home for so many people who
don't feel accepted in their families. Their bar has been a haven to
me over the years, welcoming me in and giving me friendships I
can't do without.

I led worship in a bit of a daze, trying to focus on the present
moment but with questions swirling through my head. I didn't cry,
not yet, just focused on getting through. After worship was over
at my church, I began several hours of preparation with Nigel and
JC for a vigil to be held the next day at the bar. *Of course we need to*

have a gathering to grieve. Of course we should have interfaith lead-ers. Of course you should speak, Alice. I read more news stories. The death count went up. We heard about how the police had broken through a wall to save the people left in the nightclub. I told my boss that I was leading this vigil and that it might get big. Maybe a couple hundred folks. I wrote up the plans for the vigil, when the men's chorus would sing, what Quran passage my Muslim friend would read. I revised the plans over and over as things changed. Preparation is important for these kinds of public events: you want it to go smoothly, not so you look good, but so people who come can really be present for it.

When I arrived at the bar on Monday, there were at least three hundred people already in the building. Soon, both floors of the bar were standing-room-only—four hundred people in the building. I looked over the crowd and out through the door into the street. People were there waiting to get in. That little sliver of street might have had ten people on it, I couldn't tell. We began. There were cheers sometimes—when a female trio sang "Some-where over the Rainbow," when we called all the violence in our society bullshit—and huge cheers when I said that things have changed since Stonewall forty years ago, because then the police arrested and beat the people in the bar, and now they're outside protecting us.

Between the cheers, the place was silent. They were engaged. It felt like those four hundred people were really *there*. Only there were more than four hundred. Near the end, as the men's chorus prepared to sing, I whispered to my friend Matty that I could see only a sliver of the street outside—how many were out there? He showed me a photo on his phone: the street was closed off on either end and packed full of people. There were easily another eight hundred people listening to us outside. I covered my mouth with my hand and started to cry. Matty and I clung to each other in grief for those who'd died and in awe of how many folks had come to grieve and support.

Afterward, so many people stopped me to say thank you. A group of women presented Nigel with an American flag on which they'd written all fifty of the victims' names. There were people with tears in their eyes, people who hugged, people who shook hands, people who told me about their lives. But more than that, when I walked into the bar that night, it felt like home. It had been my local bar for years, and I knew the regulars, but that night in particular, I felt like I was exactly where I was supposed to be.

This awareness is what spiritual writers call being present. Maybe the use of that word *presence* is unfamiliar to you. We use it a lot in my campus ministry—so much that my husband makes fun of me by asking me how we can be more present and intentional in, like, organizing the kids' toys or whatever. Presence is about really being where your body is—feeling the heat or cold, but also feeling your feelings, seeing your thoughts as they happen. You've probably been there at least once; it probably took you by surprise. It usually does me. *Oh, hey, I'm actually here in this moment.* We spend so much time regretting the past or being anxious about the future that we don't see the now.

It's the practice of paying attention, basically, and it really is a practice. Just like playing piano or kayaking or resolving conflict, being present requires regular practice. My daily (*cough* not really daily at all) meditation makes it more likely that I'll see or feel God acting, but doesn't actually make God show up. Preparation is part of it, but it doesn't guarantee presence.

Maybe Mary and Martha know what that's like. They were, in my mind, Jesus' chosen family. When he wanted to rest, he went to their hometown, Bethany. When their brother died, Jesus wept—one of only two places in scripture that happens. Jesus had his own family, of course—his folks, Mary and Joseph, and his brothers and sisters (it's true)—but he also had the family he'd chosen. LGBTQ folks know this concept well: the people you choose to give your heart to, not just the ones you were born with. Some people even say that it was Lazarus who was Jesus' Beloved Disciple.

There are three stories about this little family and their experi-ence of Jesus. It's hard to synthesize a single theme from them; each says something different. The stories are about gradual spiri-tual awakening, maybe. They're definitely about family life. And they circle around that experience I had of the Orlando vigil—preparation for something and presence in that something. The first Mary and Martha story is about both.

Jesus was in the living room, talking theology and politics, and Mary was in there listening and maybe arguing with him, too. Lazarus was in there, and maybe some of the disciples—Peter, James, John—hanging out, conspiring about the future. Martha was doing dishes, folding laundry, making up some hummus, and working on a spreadsheet. She got frustrated that Mary wasn't helping. "Jesus, dude, tell her she needs to help me out in here!"

Jesus said, "Martha, Martha, you're so worried and distracted. Mary's got the right idea. Come, sit."

Now, most of us now feel like Jesus is being a little bit con-descending here. Like, who's going to cook for all these people, Jesus? You want the kitchen to get roaches? Somebody has to do the routine chores that keep this ministry going, you know. But maybe Jesus wasn't saying that at all. Maybe he was saying, "We'll work that part out together in a bit. You, Martha, don't need to be relegated to the kitchen. You are a disciple, too. Come out here and be with us."

Maybe he wasn't making a value judgment; maybe he was inviting her to presence. Maybe he wasn't devaluing the prepara-tion she was doing. I know, he said "better part," but I'm think-ing it's more like she was sighing meaningfully and worried about what-ifs rather than really paying attention to what she was doing. The work she was engaged in was important, but she wasn't in it. She was in resentment and frustration and distraction. Jesus was opening up another possibility to her.

At the campus ministry where I work, one of our catchphrases is, "You are cool and fine." It comes from a meme we found online:

"What you think you are: a hot crazy truck fire mess of a person who disappoints important people. Who others think you are: cool and fine." The first time I read that, I laugh-cried. You know what that is, right? It's a kind of sudden giggle of recognition that is just as suddenly a sob. It's a reminder to us to breathe and remember that we are made in the image of God, not the image of chaos or the image of success. We are just people doing our thing. This is maybe what Jesus is saying to Martha: "You are cool and fine."

The second story is more about presence than preparation. Jesus had missed the funeral of his friend Lazarus. Martha, Lazarus's sister, heard Jesus was in town and ran to confront him, beating his chest with her fists and crying, almost screaming, "Lord, if you'd been here, my brother wouldn't have died!" Oh, that hurts: if you'd only been here, if we'd called the ambulance sooner, if I'd paid closer attention to your drinking, if only, if only.

Jesus said, "I am the Resurrection and the Life, do you believe this?"

Martha took a deep breath and said, "Yes, Lord, I believe that you are the Messiah, the Son of God, the one coming into the world."

Then Mary came running and collapsed sobbing in Jesus' arms, her eyes red and puffy, and wept, out of breath, "Lord, if you'd been here, my brother wouldn't have died." Can you feel that? Twice: "If you'd been here. . . . Why weren't you here to stop this? Where were you?"

The crowd of family and friends came following the sisters, tearing their clothing, holding one another up, and wailing. And though they didn't say it, I hear them crying, "Lord, if you'd been here, our brother wouldn't have died!"

The day I understood my brother was an alcoholic, I said, "Lord, if you had been here. . . ." I'd gone by my folks' house to pick up tables and chairs for a party at mine, and he was sitting on the couch in his bathrobe, looking a little green. When I offered to make him soup, he said it wasn't that kind of sick. I went into the kitchen to get him some water and saw a broken plate on the floor, shattered as if it had just fallen through clumsy hands, but at the same time looking abandoned, as if it had happened hours or days ago. He didn't remember it or getting home. And he was so small that day, sitting on the couch, wrapped in his robe, so small and lost. I couldn't fix it, and I couldn't protect him. Lord, if you had been here, my brother wouldn't have become an alcoholic. Lord, if you had been here.

And Jesus, realizing his mistake in missing Lazarus's funeral, suddenly felt the crushing blow of grief. He was suddenly *there*. "My friend is dead," he said. And he wept bitterly. They took him to the tomb, and he was struck by how real this death was—that coming back was no easy thing. And he longed for this grieving to be over and for his friend Lazarus. He was miserable and anxious and horrified by the smell, and he said, "Lazarus, come out!" and out came Lazarus.

At my folks' home, I swept up the plate my brother had broken, like a good Martha. I wept silently there in the kitchen for my little brother, for the part of him who died when alcohol took over, and Jesus wept with me. And I prayed that he would come out of that tomb whole and come back to us.

The third story is about preparation. It's the one everyone thinks is about Mary Magdalene (it's not) and a harlot coming to the faith (again, it's not). All four Gospels have a version of the story, and all of them are about preparation for Jesus' death. See, Jesus had come back to Bethany one last time to prepare for his looming death and was eating dinner at the family table. Mary and Martha and Lazarus were all there, eating and drinking and enjoying each other's presence.

Mary, who had a more contemplative air than the other two, got up from the table and returned with a fancy jar of perfumed oil—nard, actually, from the spikenard plant, very expensive. And it looked to be an entire pound of the stuff. It would have cost a fortune. She opened the jar, and immediately the spicy scent filled the whole house. It was intoxicating to breathe it in, like the fumes of good bourbon or fresh coffee beans, only more so. She poured handfuls of the slippery oil on Jesus' feet and wiped them with her hair. This is where some folks have said she was clearly a harlot because only a sexually sinful woman would have her hair down and perform such an intimate act with it. Only that's not the point the Gospel of John is making. Mary was foreshadowing Jesus' washing his disciples' feet at his last supper. Mary was preparing Jesus for his burial. She saw, somehow, that his end was near, so she showed him her extravagant love while he was still alive. Beautiful and heartbreaking.

This is Jesus' family of choice. These people who refill him when he has poured himself out for the crowds, the people who demand he see their loss and their grief, the people who walk with him as he walks toward his own death—these are the people Jesus chose to be his family.

I don't know if Jesus ever felt doubt while he was chatting people up in Israel. I don't know if he felt lonely or homesick. In one of the Gospels, he says, "The Son of Man has no place to lay his head." Was that said with confidence or with wistfulness? He didn't just go off by himself periodically to show off how long he could pray; he needed that time apart. Surely, though he was God incarnate, though he could just magic a bed out of the mustard seed or something, surely Jesus the man also desired the comfort of sleeping in his own bed?

Two women and their brother provided a space of rest for him, a space of refilling, like when he'd go off by himself to pray but with home-cooked meals. This family in Bethany you wouldn't have expected in first-century Israel—women running a household, making extravagant choices—he gave them a deeper, more divine relationship with God simply by being present with them, and a kind of consecration of their daily lives. Mary and Martha and Lazarus gave him—reminded him of, maybe—an awareness of God's presence. Yes, I know he's God, but also he's human, and

I imagine all the preaching and healing and pushing back against authority gave him a hell of a headache.

Jesus feels our own headaches now from dealing with the world. He understands how LGBTQ folks form new families around themselves because their families of origin cannot find the grace to love them. He understands how kids who survived the foster system create new families so they won't be alone. Jesus understands choosing family outside of the ones who birthed us. My family is both. I choose the people who made me because they're amazing and I'm constantly aware of what a gift that is. I choose the people who choose me—my siblings at Below Zero, my house church. And Mary and Martha chose Jesus to be in their family.

I said at the beginning that the vigil at the bar showed me I was where I was supposed to be. That feeling—of rightness, of belonging, of family—is Jesus showing up in our lives.

Herodias and Herodias

Not So Sexy after All

> When his daughter Herodias came in and danced, she pleased Herod and his guests; and the king said to the girl, "Ask me for whatever you wish, and I will give it." And he solemnly swore to her, "Whatever you ask me, I will give you, even half of my kingdom."
>
> —Mark 6:22–23

I left the theater, my first vocational love, for the church because there was too much politics in the theatre. The church, surely, would be a place of transparency, where people leave manipulation at the door, I thought. Go ahead and giggle at my naïveté. I'll wait.

Church politics is not taught in seminary. How do you affirm the sacredness of the sanctuary and worship elements to the altar guild and also advocate for the youth to play capture the flag in the same space? How do you run a building campaign to get much-needed space for mission and not play favorites with the wealthy donors? And how do we exist as a spiritual body in a secular world, where our thoughts about compassion and unity and justice are looked at with doubt, given our history of violence? What if one Sunday I'm preaching on the prophets who were notoriously offensive to their listeners, and I want to swear in my sermon to reflect that?

My motto as a preacher is, "Say the thing; keep getting paid." Because I like to have a house to live in and food to eat, plus I adore my job on campus, so I need to not be totally outrageous and get fired. But playing it safe is not the way of God, as far as I can tell. I have to speak the truth and speak it in such a way that the congregation will hear it, two not inconsequential tasks. If the Gospel this week is Jesus saying that rich people will have a very hard time being part of God's kingdom, then I kind of need to say that. I mean, of course there's good news, but it doesn't always feel that way. All people being part of a divine equalizing sounds great if you're poor or oppressed, but it sounds like a threat if you're the one with money or power. Truth-telling is hard.

So we know there's politics in the church; there always has been. Popes used to consecrate kings, and clergy still wield a tremendous amount of political power. How women wield power, political or otherwise, has often been more subtle, because for long stretches of time, we didn't have any—officially, anyway.

We didn't invent politics in the twentieth century. *The West Wing* didn't invent rejecting the premise of the question. We didn't invent shifting loyalties and evolving opinions. We didn't invent politically expedient marriages or wars over land or hurt feelings. Beside prostitution, politics might be the world's oldest profession. Reading the histories of the Herod family—and the Maccabees, did you know they were related?—is like reading a newspaper now, only slightly more bloody.

The first thing you need to know about Herod's family—the huge dynasty of which Herod the Great was something of a patriarch—is that they were incredibly uncreative when it came to names. There are two men named Antipater, and almost all of the men in the family were called Herod, either as their first name or later as an honorific for being in the family. Herod Philip married his father Herod's great-niece Herodias. They named their daughter Herodias as well but helpfully nicknamed her Salome to avoid confusion. Then Herodias the Elder divorced Herod Philip to marry his brother Herod Antipas. The family tree has a lot of unhealthily overlapping branches.

Herodias and her second husband, Herod Antipas, had big shoes to fill when they came to the throne. For one thing, he wasn't actually king, because the Roman occupiers didn't think he had the chops. And compared with his dad, Herod the Great, he didn't. Dad had been the intimate friend of Mark Antony, Cleopatra, and Caesar Augustus. He had been a brutal and intensely paranoid king but also incredibly effective. Herod the Great had built lots of cities from nothing, had spent years wrangling an era of tense peace in Palestine, and had political clout. Though not beloved by the people, he was respected by them—mostly. I mean, he did have people killed who got in his way. Or who he thought were going to get in his way. At any rate, his nickname "the Great" was well earned. In contrast, Herod Antipas, Herodias's husband, could have been "Herod the Just Okay."

This Herod had been married to a princess from the neighboring country of Nabotea, but he sent her packing when he met his brother's wife, Herodias. Herodias was captivating—intelligent, wily, beautiful, ambitious. The princess of Nabotea returned to her family, who took none too kindly to the divorce. And when I say "none too kindly," I of course mean they prepared themselves for war. Like you do. This Herod tried to play politics with Rome as his father had—shifting his loyalties at just the right time, offering ridiculously lavish gifts, and naming cities after powerful friends. He just wasn't as good at it. And then there's the matter of John the Baptizer.

John was Jesus' weird, loud cousin. He was a bit of a zealot and possibly a seditionist. He'd been preaching out in the countryside about the evils of this modern era, with specific loving care given to those terrible people in power who exploit the proletariat, who, by the way, are also pretty terrible, kind of like snakes, ugh. He also had a sermon about the evils of second marriages when the first husband is still alive; yes, I'm talking to you,

Herod and Herodias, why do you ask? Scripture is not entirely clear about whether it was the whiff of incest around her marrying two brothers or whether it was the poor form of the divorce. John also preached about another king who would come after him to change everything (*cough* Jesus), which you would think would be the threat Herod and Herodias would worry about. But Herod liked John and found him both holy and perplexing. I imagine them staying up nights over bottles of wine, talking of philosophy and dames.

Herodias did not like John. It was embarrassing for people to hear him say she was a whore and not a good Jew. It was awkward because she had indeed abandoned her husband for his brother, but Herod Philip was going nowhere fast, and didn't she have a right to make the life she wanted? Didn't she have the political acumen to shape events behind the scenes, to help Herod become king and not just tetrarch? Couldn't she, as a queen, wield real power and bring even more stability to her country? Cozying up to the enemy is not how we win. John's sanctimonious and, frankly, nut-job sermons were not helpful to their image with the people. John the Baptizer was a voice crying out in the wilderness to destabilize their reign, and people were listening.

So Herodias called on her daughter Herodias, also known as Salome, for help. Mother and daughter were both implicated in John's preaching, and they worked out a plan to remove the obstacle from their path. If she couldn't order his death herself and couldn't be seen asking for it, she could manipulate it—which was no different from any of the men's manipulations and compromises happening all around them. Salome would dance before Herod and all his friends at his birthday party. This would not be a cute tap dance by a little girl to make her stepfather say, "Awww," and offer her a toy. Salome was nineteen and likely married. She was a woman acquainted with the glories and uses of her body. She was still young enough to have a firm, smooth body that jiggled in all the right places. She was ambitious like her mother, and though she wished for more conventional power, she was willing to use the tools she had.

It was risky, and even the idea of Salome offering herself up at the feast might have made the two of them a little sick. *What if things got out of hand? How far would she go? Who would protect her?* But they knew the power of the female body to the men in their family, so they did it.

The night of Herod's birthday, the party was well under way. Meats and pastries were piled on the tables, and wine flowed freely. Musicians played the smooth jazz and hot adult contemporary of the era. Other dancers spun around the room, their scarves brushing across the heads or laps of the feasting men. Salome appeared in an archway, and the music haltingly quieted. Conversation ceased; cutlery dropped to plates. In the stillness, Salome's kohl-outlined eyes gazed at Herod's with intention. Without saying a word, she told him this was for him.

We know this in legend as the "Dance of the Seven Veils," the first striptease. It probably wasn't. The first, that is. It was definitely a tease, whether she stripped down or not. As she began to move, the scarves draping her body swayed and hinted at curves beneath. She leaped and swayed, arching her back to lift her breasts as a gift. She spun and beckoned the onlookers to feast their eyes on her body. She moved in and out of pools of light, hiding as much as she revealed. Perhaps she danced behind Herod himself, sliding her hands down his body and encouraging him to think there was more to his birthday present. Perhaps she exposed her body to him, making him salivate for what her mother could not offer him.

When she finished, the room exploded into applause and shouts. Herod, face flushed with pleasure—maybe drunk, maybe just proud of the alliance he'd made with the two Herodiases and feeling expansive on his birthday—offered her a gift: "Anything you like, my dear, worth up to even half of my realm." Could he really be as unsuspecting as that? Did he not know his wife nor the centuries-long game between men and women? But no, Herod was only the latest in a line of men who made deals without considering the consequences. Remember Jephtha in the book of Judges promising God a human sacrifice in return for a military victory that had already been promised him? He promised to sacrifice the first person he saw when he arrived home, and who came out that door but his radiant daughter. Herod's kingly arousal was about to fail.

Salome replied to Herod's offer, "Gosh, I don't know what to ask for." It's unlikely she was particularly innocent here. She went to her mother to confirm what they had decided upon. "Be strong," her mother said. Or maybe, "Let's get the bastard." Or even, "I can't believe that worked." Salome returned to Herod and the party, and in a clear, resonant voice, eyes flashing, she said, "I want John the Baptizer's head on a platter."

And Herod, having sworn a public oath to do what she asked and apparently not wanting to upset his guests, did the "honorable" thing and had John killed. Salome took John's head on its platter to her mother, blood staining her skin and the scarves she'd worn to seduce Herod. Herodias got what she wanted: a troublemaker neutralized and the path to stability and power clear.

This image of Salome holding John the Baptizer's head or of her offering it to Herodias is a common theme in art history. Along with Judith decapitating Holofernes and Jael driving a tent peg through Sisera's skull, artists delight in imagining women taking their vengeance on abusers. But it's not as empowering as you might think. In the Middle Ages in particular, the trope was called "the power of woman," and it signified sarcasm. "Look how hilarious it is that women could have this kind of power over men. Aren't they cute?" it said to viewers. "It must be that time of the month, am I right?" How could these women have possibly had their own motivations and righteous indignation?

But Herodias and Herodias weren't hysterical women enacting evil plans, and they weren't powerless either. They were just people—people with power and privilege, to be sure, and certainly people who wielded the power in the way Samuel long ago warned the Israelites that kings would. Herodias and Herodias and their husbands used their political power to get shit done. Should they have? No, that's too simplistic a question, and any answer to it isn't helpful. Constantine, first Christian ruler of the Roman Empire, and later Queen Elizabeth I of England played these games with the church, using it as a tool to stabilize the realm. "Should" isn't the right question.

We could just as easily ask now, "How do we get done what we want to get done? How do we play politics to further God's justice in the world? How much brutality and sacrifice of our own bodies do we allow even now to do what needs to be done? And could there be another way?" John the Baptizer and his cousin Jesus stood up to Herod and Herodias and spoke truth to them that there were other ways of finding stability and power—that even power itself was suspect.

Popular history suggests that the Dance of the Seven Veils was about sex and that it gives us a peep show into the immoral opponents of early Christianity. What it's really about is how we compromise ourselves to get justice, or at least something that looks like justice. It's about women using the power they have, unrecognized by the ruling authority, to make their marks on the world. And it's about how politics is a dance, hiding as much as it reveals.

Priscilla and Phoebe and Lydia and Rhoda

Paul's Church Ladies

Paul said farewell to the believers and sailed for Syria, accompanied by Priscilla and Aquila.

—Acts 18:18

G rowing up, I always thought of the ladies in my dad's churches like the Dowager Countess in *Downton Abbey*—Maggie Smith at her accomplished, pinched, disapproving best. I felt like I was too young or too crazy for them. After a couple of years in the choir, I began to pay more attention; I saw they were sweet and caring and committed to the church. They were the ones crawling around on their knees with brown paper and an iron to get the wax out of the carpet. They were the ones bringing casseroles when someone was sick. They were the ones praying hard every night for me and the other teenagers, and for all I know, the power of their prayers is why nothing really bad happened to us. They were the ones holding together the fragile conglomeration of broken people we call the church.

We so often think of the early church as the domain of the twelve male apostles and of Saint Paul. Those men are the ones named in the Gospels, the ones asking the often-dumb questions, the ones present at the resurrection appearances on the beach and in the upper room. But at the very least, who cooked for them? You know as well as I do that Mary Magdalene and others were around Jesus and the twelve constantly. Mary Magdalene is the only one that all four Gospels consistently mention being present at the empty tomb. *Of course there were women in the early church,* we say to ourselves, but what does that mean? Were they all getting wax out of folks' robes, or were any of them actively spreading the gospel like Peter and Paul?

Even though Paul says women shouldn't speak in church, he names a bunch of them as church leaders: Junia, Julia, Tryphena, Tryphosa, Mary, Claudia, Damaris, Drusilla, Persis, Chloe, Lydia, Euodia, Synthyche, and the "elect lady" to whom 2 John was written—the only biblical book directly addressed to a woman. They're spoken of in the book of Acts, in Paul's writings, and in the Paul fan fiction. (Paul for sure wrote seven letters included in the Christian scriptures, but there are fourteen with his name on them. Because of the way they're written—certain words used or not used, differing theological concepts—we think the other seven were written by his students and fans asking, "What would Paul do?" Therefore, fan fiction.) Some of these women are only referred to, while others have more extensive stories.

Priscilla was married to Aquila, and this rhyming couplet traveled with Paul around bits of the Mediterranean. The three of them were tentmakers, transient entrepreneurs who shared the good news of Jesus with the folks they met. They were a bit like the circuit-riding preachers of early American Christianity, moving from place to place, meeting people, talking about Jesus, eating Jell-O salad at potlucks, and then moving on to the next town. Funny story: the Greek word for their profession translated "tentmaker" is very similar to the ancient word for "theater set designer." My dad—a priest and, coincidentally, theater set designer—has often remarked upon this similarity. I love it. Paul and Priscilla and Aquila weren't making tents for people in the marketplace; they

were itinerant theater techies, wandering the Mediterranean, ply-
ing their trade as artists, spreading the drama of Jesus' good news
and of Aeschylus. Maybe.

We don't know much more than that about Priscilla and
Aquila, but I like to imagine them arguing theology with Jews and
Gentiles alike, right alongside Paul. "Of course we are justified by
grace alone," Priscilla would say. "Look at my husband, Aquila.
He's a good man, but every time he doesn't put his dishes in the
dishwasher and they get all crusty is a point against him. There's
no way to recover from that." Or arguing with Paul the way I wish
I could. "Brother Paul," she might have said, "What's this about it
being shameful for a woman to speak in church?" Some folks even
think she wrote the book of Hebrews.

But there are no heroic deeds attributed to Priscilla, no transcendent appearances of God in the desert. She went about her
life, praying and cooking, speaking and tentmaking.

Now, Phoebe was Paul's patron, one of those women whose
names are written in huge typeface on the banners at fund-raising
galas—you know, "Angel Donors: Dr. and Mrs. Charles Smith-
erington" or similar. She and others provided food and lodging
to these fascinating, difficult, spiritual men. They found ways to
be near them, to hear their parables and arguments. Phoebe used
what she had to support these traveling preachers and, by exten-
sion, support the men and women who came to hear them.

Phoebe was Paul's benefactor and was, it turns out, a deacon
herself. She held the same office that Timothy, one of Paul's closest lieutenants, did: *diakonos*, or servant. That was the same term
that Paul even used to describe himself. These three were servants
of God, servants of the people they preached to, servants in both
action and title. Phoebe is the only woman recorded in scripture
to bear that title, though I doubt very much that she was the only
woman in that era to do so. When Paul wrote to Timothy (or,
rather, when one of Paul's fans wrote to Timothy), he spilled a
lot of ink describing the conduct of deacons—their honesty,

generosity, sobriety, and all—and wrote specifically that women in that role ought to meet the same standard.

Phoebe was one of this company of faithful leaders. She sat with other women and heard their joys and sorrows. She heard their confessions. At their baptisms, Phoebe was there to anoint them with the cross of Christ. Deacon Phoebe had only a brief mention in scripture but was remembered long after her death. Three hundred years later, her name was invoked on another female deacon's gravestone: "Sophia, a deacon, a second Phoebe." We don't know anything about this second Phoebe, but as when we call someone "another Mother Theresa," we know that whoever uses such language sees the named person—and therefore the one who follows her—as someone special. We know that the footsteps she followed were celebrated indeed.

But there are no heroic deeds attributed to Phoebe, no walking with God in the Garden of Eden. She went about her life, praying and benefacting, speaking and listening.

Lydia was an ancient Middle Eastern fashion designer. She was known for the purple cloth she made—purple for royalty, purple for wealth, because it was such a difficult color to dye. Lydia was a woman of money and substance; the business she owned kept her comfortable, and her mind kept her engaged with the world. When Paul and Silas and Timothy came to her town, they went down to the river to pray with the women. They spoke their piece and praised God, and Lydia's mind was open to their message. She heard them and knew that this was what she'd been waiting for. She said to them, "Brothers, you have fed me with your words; let me feed you at my table." She said, "But would you baptize me and my daughters now, here in this river?"

They did and she did. But there are no heroic deeds attributed to Lydia, no wrestling an angel to receive a blessing. She went about her life, praying and listening, selling and leading.

Rhoda couldn't contain her excitement. Peter had been arrested by Herod (the Just Okay) for preaching the Christian gospel, for sedition—and just because, really. He had been bound in two chains between two guards behind a locked door guarded by another two guards. Just a tad overkill. An angel had appeared to him and led him out from prison, the doors opening in front of them like magic, and no one the wiser.

After this miraculous exodus, Peter went to his friend Mary's house. Not that Mary. And not that one either. A whole other Mary. He knocked on the door, and the maid Rhoda said, "Who's there?" "Pete," he said. "Pete who?" "Pete-zza delivery! Ha! No, wait, come back. . . ." But she was gone, so excited that their friend Peter had been sprung from prison that she didn't even let him in. She ran to her mistress and was so overcome with happy dancing and laughter that everyone thought she'd gone crazy. Meanwhile, Peter continued knocking, regretting his terrible joke and hoping someone would let him in soon.

Rhoda, her story quite short, has no heroic deeds attributed to her and no Jesus appearing at a well to talk theology. She went about her life, praying and serving, laundering and laughing.

These women and so many others haven't had epic, fantastic experiences of God recorded for posterity. Their experiences of God were quotidian, ordinary. God was there helping them to be ready to hear and help. God was there with them, encouraging them as they made breakfast or disciplined their kids or traded in the marketplace. God sat with them in their sorrows just as they sat with others. There may be no heroic deeds attributed to them, yet they were heroes of the faith.

And maybe there are no heroic deeds attributed to you or me. We go about our lives—taking kids or grandkids to music lessons, taking out the trash, organizing departments of people, teaching fifth-grade math, or ironing the linens at church. We don't often have burning-bush moments. Maybe that's not because they don't happen but because we're not really present to see them.

One of my most favorite theologians, Kathleen Norris, writes that one of her first experiences in an Episcopal church made her giggle with recognition. After everyone filed up to receive Communion, she watched the priest take water and ceremonially wash the dishes in front of everyone. It's something we do in liturgical churches—we eat the meal, even if it's just a bit of bread and a sip of wine, and then the priest drinks the remaining wine, pours water onto the plate and into the cup, and then drinks that as well. It's not a real dishwashing, of course—the altar guild does a much better job of that later—but it's symbolic. And Norris was delighted that in the midst of something as holy and centering, even heroic, as Communion, there was the everydayness of eating a meal and washing the dishes.

I get so caught up in my day-to-day worries that burning-bush moments catch me completely off guard. They're like the day I was crisscrossing campus, visiting various offices, meeting with students, and I happened to look up and then couldn't look away. I lay down on the grass in the quad and just stared at the cloudless, ridiculously blue sky. I thought, "How is this color even real?" It was so beautiful and pure, and I know it sounds a little odd, but my lungs just opened up, and I felt like I could breathe again. So I did. Several deep breaths later, I felt God there with me, holding my limbs to the earth and filling my lungs with air. It wasn't that all my worries were gone, but they kind of fell into place. "I am where I'm supposed to be, and so are you," I thought. It was sacred and ordinary ground.

Strangely (or maybe not so strangely), I find spiritual focus in hanging laundry out to dry on my clothesline. I have one of those umbrella dryers that spin in the wind. I take a couple of loads of wet laundry out and stand in the sunlight, hanging diapers and shirts and thinking about God. The sun is on my skin, and there's sometimes a breeze in my hair and smells from tomato plants and roses in my nose. Later I come take the clothes down, and they're stiff and dry and smell of outside—not the fake "balmy breeze" scent in fabric softener, but actual outside. I have taken a basket of wet laundry outside after arguments with my kids or husband or after a truly damnable day, and after I'm done stabbing the clothespins over the laundry, I've been able to breathe again. It's the most prosaic thing in the world and yet, for me, the most transcendent.

Artist Makoto Fujimura thinks this is precisely what Jesus meant when he told us to consider the lilies. Jesus seems to suggest we should just not worry; before bringing up lilies, he said worrying about the future doesn't make it safer or longer. So consider the lilies and how worry-free they are. Be more like the flowers, which don't work or worry, and aren't they beautiful? (Thanks, Jesus, that's helpful. I'll be like a flower, and my mortgage will pay for itself.) In contrast to that interpretation, Fujimura wonders if Jesus meant for us to go consider the lilies: Feeling stressed? Go look at some flowers. Or the sunrise through clouds. Or waves rolling in at low tide. Just staring at a tree or some daisies might help us breathe again and recognize God's work in the world. This is particularly profound, I think, because we all get caught up thinking it's our work alone in the world. We will fix everything that's broken if we just worry and work hard enough. But we are not in control of it, we are involved.

I know this peace in ordinariness is not the everyday experience of all the world. My idyllic little backyard laundry moment is naive when compared with someone experiencing an abusive partner or leaving home as a refugee or dying of whatever stupid thing is killing us now. Hate and fear and insecurity overwhelm and make the possibility of God's presence seem distant or fictional. Considering the lilies or doing the spiritual dishes or making tents doesn't take away the pain. But each of these responses do make the pain bearable. They make it smaller than it looks.

Albert Camus is not often considered a prophet of hope, given the meaninglessness he writes about. And though the following quotation is questionably attributed to him on the internet, it does sum up his perspective neatly: "The only way to deal with an unfree world is to become so absolutely free that your very existence is an act of rebellion." Even in the midst of impossible situations, we can find freedom and room to breathe. Women in concentration camps during World War II wrote down recipes for their favorite dishes and for fanciful, made-up ones on whatever scraps of paper they could find. Surrounded by sorrow and death, they reached for joy. Priscilla and Phoebe and Lydia and Rhoda certainly did not have perfectly safe and beautiful lives, but they lived that rebellious freedom.

Priscilla and Phoebe and Lydia and Rhoda are the original church ladies—the Eunices and Carols and Nancyes who I once thought of as terrifying and who hold us together. These early church ladies didn't meet and probably didn't even know of each other's existence. They were and are apostles, deacons, leaders of house churches, and volunteers of the year. Church ladies of every generation might not have looked like burning bushes, but their hearts and lives were aflame with the Spirit.

Mary of Magdala

Who Lives, Who Dies, Who Tells Your Story?

> When she had said this, she turned around and saw Jesus standing there, but she did not know that it was Jesus. Jesus said to her, "Woman, why are you weeping? For whom are you looking?" Supposing him to be the gardener, she said to him, "Sir, if you have carried him away, tell me where you have laid him, and I will take him away." Jesus said to her, "Mary!" She turned and said to him in Hebrew, "Rabbouni!" (which means Teacher).
>
> —JOHN 20:14–16

Mary Magdalene was not a prostitute. She was not Mary of Bethany, sister of Martha and Lazarus. Mary did not anoint Jesus' feet with fancy oil, did not weep dramatically over his feet, and did not wipe them with her hair.

She said something like this every time she met someone new and they got that speculative look in their eyes. "I should have a T-shirt made," she thought. "You're thinking of a different Mary, I'm afraid," she said apologetically. "I'm the one who went to the tomb when everyone else had run away and who helped fund the whole ministry. Does that ring a bell?"

I imagine she wasn't offended by being thought of as a former prostitute. Some of the people in her community were sex workers—some by choice, some out of desperation or force—and they were loving, complex people. It's just that she wasn't; that was something put on her by someone who didn't like what she was doing, intending the label as an insult. And it's not that she didn't like being associated with Mary of Bethany's grief and gratitude. It's just that it's not her story.

Another story people tell about her is that she met Tiberius Caesar at a dinner party and accidentally invented Easter eggs. Supposedly she was telling ol' Caesar about Jesus and happened to have an egg in her hand while she gesticulated (no, we don't know if Mary Magdalene talked with her hands, but I like to think so). Caesar laughed and said her story was as likely as the egg she was waving around turning red. Which it promptly did. And that's why, kids, we dye eggs on Easter. And even that whole story is about as likely as the one about candy canes being about Jesus' blood, which is to say, not bloody likely.

Some other folks say that as she neared death, angels carried her up into heaven seven times a day and fed her. And then they brought her back here afterward, I guess, which would suck if you think about it. There's a monastery in Greece that says it has her preserved left hand, that the hand is incorruptible (smells like flowers and is still soft and pliable), and that it works miracles. I mean, it's not that these things *couldn't* have happened. People understood her as being a VIP, and VIPs must have intense, unbelievable stories associated with them.

Lots of people over the years have said Mary Magdalene was married to Jesus. I worked at a national chain bookstore the whole time *The Da Vinci Code* was on the best-seller list. So many folks who bought it asked me in awe if I'd known that Mary and Jesus had been married, and how could the church have covered this up for so long? They also asked me what I thought about Emperor Constantine inventing the Patriarchy. (Which he didn't, just to be clear. Patriarchy had been around, kicking ass and taking names, since before Noah was a boy.) Look, could Mary Magdalene have been Jesus' wife? Sure. It would have been a little odd for a thirty-year-old rabbinic student not to have been married, and some commentators speculate that the wedding Jesus and his mother attended at Cana was his own. But it's unlikely. There were many celibate prophets and rabbis at the time. And it's kind of not the point of either Jesus' ministry or of Mary Magdalene's life. That's not her story. She has her own story.

She was just this woman living her life, not a cosmic divine feminine and not a tragic whore triumphantly overcoming her terrible past. Mary Magdalene was ordinary. Ordinary the way my friends who are recovering addicts are ordinary. People who engage with addiction-recovery programs and get sober are often put up on pedestals for being so damned brave and strong and heroic. But they'd be the first to say clearly that they aren't. They're just working through one day at a time. I expect Mary Magdalene was like my friends Vicky and Tom (not their real names), who when you tell them you respect them for the hard work they're doing, brush it off. They have to, because making what they're doing exceptional makes it that much harder to maintain. They have had to find a new normal, a new story to tell, just as Mary Magdalene did after she met Jesus. Not because she was a notorious sinner—at least, no more than you or I—but because Jesus changed everything.

She was there at the beginning, or almost the beginning anyway. Before any of these stories about her were committed to paper, she'd heard a new rabbi speaking to a crowd about how their poverty and grief and insignificance were blessings. She'd thought, "That doesn't even make sense." She'd stopped and listened and been overcome by the poetry and—and—incisiveness of his words. They felt like they could cut through reality itself and remake it into something beautiful and tender. "We could change the world if we lived that way," she thought. She waited until the crowd got bored and dispersed before approaching the rabbi. "I heard your speech," she said. "Did you really mean all that? Because if you did, I'm in."

Rabbi Jesus had looked at her intently and then said quietly, almost as an afterthought, "Come out of her." Something poured out of her like air rushing out of her lungs and also not like that at all, leaving her shaking and wide awake, cheeks wet with tears. The something that left her was legion (they called it demons at the time): her self-hatred, her driving need to be right, her inability to forgive her brother, the phantom pain that had caused her to limp. Whatever they were, the things that had plagued her for years—they were gone. This Rabbi Jesus had healed her and, to put it mildly, was something more than a rabbi.

So Mary joined the disciples, the band of dusty, talkative, painfully earnest men whom the Rabbi Jesus had inexplicably chosen. They wandered from town to town, eating and drinking when they could, sleeping rough sometimes, other times in the houses of friends or family. Mary listened intently to Jesus' stories and bit her lip mischievously when he won verbal fights with the religious authorities. I like to imagine a smirk on her face, because that's what I do when I read about Jesus throwing down with the religious authorities. "Bunch of pinched old windbags," she thought. "Serves them right for telling us all we're doing it wrong. Taste of your own medicine, friends?" When Jesus healed the blind and sick, she smiled at them and cried in delighted disbelief with them, wondering "How can this be real?"

Mary did her part for their little family. She came from money, or anyway she had some—more than enough to cover their expenses, particularly since there were several other women who did the same. They sat around the fire at night, the women philanthropists, their eyes reflecting the flames, the flames reflecting their hearts. They talked about where they might go next and whether they'd be able to get fresh fish and leeks for dinner. They talked about servanthood, how it felt to give away the money that protected them. They talked about revolution and freedom and pain. They talked about Jesus' wild new take on the law. "Love the Lord your God with all your heart, your soul, your mind, and your strength, and your neighbor as yourself," he said, which wasn't new at all, but when he talked about neighbors and about love, their minds opened up like arms opening for an embrace. There was so much more in the story Jesus was telling about the world than they'd ever thought.

Much later, after the supper that turned out to be their last, after Judas (God, what was up with that guy?) had left and returned with soldiers, after the other disciples had lost faith and scattered, Mary and the other women stayed outside the prison, praying, weeping, and discussing what all this could mean. "What would Jesus say?" they wondered, and not a one of them could answer.

She was there at the end. Mary was one of three or four women off to the side, watching the crucifixion. There's some question about how many of them were there (because of exciting grammar reasons), but there they were at the bottom of the hill called Skull. They bore witness to what was happening, tears flowed down some of their faces, and others breathed deeply and slowly through their noses to keep the emotions under control. They muttered prayers and deprecations under their breath and waited for something to happen—for angels to take him down from the cross, or for the heavens to open up, or for the soldiers to strip themselves naked and run away. Anything so this torment would end. They did not move their eyes from their friend and Lord until he died in front of them. I imagine Mary Magdalene being like my mother-in-law planning funerals or weddings or lunch on Tuesday: with a million questions still within her but squaring her shoulders, straightening her veil, and saying, "Right. We have mouths to feed and a body to bury. Let's get to it."

And she was there at the next beginning. A day and a half after Jesus died, Mary and some of the other women—different ones are named in the stories, as though we can't quite remember, but Mary Magdalene is always there—got up before the sun,

dressed themselves, and picked up their jars of perfumes and oint-
ments for Jesus' body. The wealth they had used to support Jesus'
ministry they now used to honor him in death. As they came to
the cave where he was buried, the sun just peeked over the hill
in front of them, spilling brilliant light everywhere, extravagantly,
wastefully. It was so beautiful and so sad that Mary cried, her tears
falling extravagantly, wastefully.

They ducked their heads into the cave and found nothing.
Emptiness. Jesus was gone.

In John's version, Mary ran back into town in a panic to Peter
and John and told them what she'd seen: "Someone's stolen the
body. It's gone. Why would someone do that? Why?" Together they
ran back, anxiety in their stomachs urging them on. The two men
saw the emptiness and left, suddenly understanding something of
what Jesus had said about resurrection and rejoicing. Mary, bless
her, hadn't yet made the connection, and she wept as she reentered
the tomb. There she saw two people she couldn't quite look at,
one at each end of the outcropping where Jesus' body had been.
They said, "Why are you crying?" She said, "Someone has taken
my friend's body," and stumbled away from the cave, mind swirling with questions. In her haste, she tripped, and someone caught
her by the waist, raising her up. She looked at him and figured he
must be the gardener, come to weed and prune and harvest. She
wasn't wrong, precisely. But not expecting to see Jesus, she didn't.
He said, "Why are you crying? Who are you looking for?" She said
again, "Someone has taken my friend's body." The gardener said,
"Mary." And finally she saw him, as he'd seen her the day they met.
"Rabbi," she breathed.

Mary had lots of theological questions, mostly around "What
the hell does this mean? I mean, really, though." She went back
into town, slower this time, pondering in her heart what to say.
When she found the other disciples again, she said, "What we
know, what we saw, is that our friend died. He was put in a tomb
with a heavy stone across the front. We were devastated. When we

went back this morning, he wasn't there anymore. And then we met him on the road. What do we do with that?"

Because Mary Magdalene was the first to see Jesus the Christ at the resurrection, because she was the one to tell the others, scholars call her "apostle to the apostles." But she was, straight up, the first apostle. Or, really, she was the first Christian—the first person to see Jesus' resurrection and the first to tell someone else.

Mary Magdalene's name has come to mean many things. Her surname—Magdalene, "from Magdala"—transformed over the years into *maudlin*, meaning weepy in a sappy, overly dramatic sort of way, mostly because folks still identified her with the weeping woman who washed Jesus' feet with her hair. Still not that Mary. But she did weep, quite a lot actually. Dozens of icons and paintings depict her in a posture of grief.

She wept for Jesus at the crucifixion, grieving the loss of her friend. Where was God?

She wept for the disciples' hopes that Jesus would change things. Where was that beautiful vision of the world he talked about?

She wept for the boys in her village conscripted into the army and the families working themselves to death even to eat.

She wept for the destruction of the temple, for her people in captivity in Babylon remembering their song, "We sat and wept, and wept, for thee Zion," and for her people enslaved in Egypt.

She wept for Cain killing his brother Abel and for Eve's grief.

She wept for joy when Ruth and Naomi found security and when the lovers in the Song of Songs found each other.

When our friends and coworkers can't speak up for themselves and when our corporations get away with exploitation, Mary Magdalene weeps with us.

When we hear our children whimper in pain or sadness, Mary Magdalene weeps with us.

When yet another shooter opens fire in a crowd, when yet another black man is shot by police, when yet more police are shot themselves, Mary Magdalene weeps with us.

She weeps with us when all we have is tears, tearing us up from the inside. She weeps with us when we can't, when all we have is shock or numbness.

A year ago, a friend attempted suicide. He had received word that he was going to be sent to prison because he'd violated his probation, and he was terrified. He called me that night to say good-bye. I thought he meant "good-bye" because the prison was out of state and, you know, it was prison. But the tone of his voice and the silence after I said I'd miss him told me he meant a different kind of good-bye. He didn't confirm or deny, and I asked him not to, didn't think he really would, but I didn't blame him either. He's on the sex offender registry, and while his original offense wasn't completely depraved, it doesn't matter. His years of therapy and self-transformation didn't matter. He would have no future. He said his mother was there with him, and he had to go. After we hung up, I fell apart, tears and snot flowing freely as I sobbed for his misery and for a world where he could find no hope.

He survived his attempted suicide. He was not sent to prison. And months later, he told me haltingly that he was glad he had survived, that on the other side of death he saw possibility. It's not all sunrise and flowers. Because of his past, he's got a long road to walk. But there's something new happening, something he couldn't see while he stood with Mary at the foot of the hill called the Skull.

Mary's tears at the tomb are recognition that this world ends in death. That was the end of the story—a tragedy, not a comedy. She wept at the tomb first in grief but then in surprise and recognition. "He is not dead, he is alive!" And then she continued on, squaring her shoulders, not ignoring the pain but confronting it. Other people told her story, getting the details wrong but remembering her there at the beginning and at the end and at the new beginning. Mary told her story of meeting Jesus to others, tears still fresh on her cheeks, and possibility in her heart.

Appendix A

The Biblical Stories Themselves and Where to Find Them

Maybe you'd like to read the stories for yourself and come to your own conclusions. Please, be my guest. Here is a list of references for the stories you just read.

Tamar. Genesis 38.

Rahab. Joshua 2 and 6.

Bathsheba. 2 Samuel 11–12.

Ruth. Ruth (the whole book, it's not that long—4 chapters—you can do it).

Mary Theotokos. For the annunciation and birth of Jesus, Matthew 1–2 and Luke 1–2. For her presence at the crucifixion, Matthew 27; Mark 15; John 19. For her presence with the disciples after the ascension, Acts 1–2.

Asherah. Deuteronomy 16:21; Judges 3:7; Judges 6; 1 Kings 15:9–15; 1 Kings 16:31–33; 1 Kings 18:17–40; much of 2 Kings; 2 Chronicles 15.

Eve. Genesis 1–3.

Hagar. Genesis 16–21.

Deborah and Jael. Judges 4–5.

Song of Songs. Song of Songs 1–8.

Widows. 1 Kings 17; Luke 2; Luke 7; Titus 2:3–5. For references in the prophets, Isaiah 10:1–3; Jeremiah 22:1–5; Ezekiel 22:6–7; Psalm 68:5–6, among others.

Jerusalem. Ezekiel 16 and 23.

Susanna. Susanna and other additions to the book of Daniel, found in the Apocrypha.

Woman at the Well. John 4.

Woman on the Road. Matthew 15:21–28; Mark 7:24–30.

Mary and Martha. For the anointing, Matthew 26:6–13; Mark 14:3–9; Luke 7:36–50; John 12:1–8. For complaints that their brother wouldn't have died, John 11. For the one who chose the better part, Luke 10: 38–42.

Herodias and Herodias. Matthew 14; Mark 6; Luke 3.

Priscilla. Acts 18.

Phoebe. Romans 16.

Lydia. Acts 16.

Rhoda. Acts 12.

Mary Magdalene. For the healing from demons, Luke 8. For her presence at the crucifixion, Matthew 27; Mark 15; John 19. For her witness of the resurrection, Matthew 28; Mark 16; Luke 24; John 20.

Appendix B

Homework: a.k.a. Ideas for Further Reading

You say you want to delve deeper into this surprising world of biblical women? Well, I'm definitely not the first to write about them, nor the last. There's a lot of crap out there, though, so here are a few suggestions to get you started.

Farrell, Heather. *Women in the Scriptures* (blog), womeninthescriptures.com, accessed August 29, 2016.

> Blog by a Mormon woman with some extensive lists of women in the Bible and her thoughts about them. Definitely from a more conservative bent.

Garcia, Magaly. "Yes, Women Can Be Apostles, Too." *Sojourners*, May 17, 2016, https://sojo.net/articles/keeping-feast/yes-women -can-be-apostles-too.

> The title of this article says it all. Also, *Sojourners* is pretty cool.

Harris, Stephen L. *Understanding the Bible.* London: Mayfield, 2002.

> Although this is not feminist per se, it's a straightfor- ward look at what's in the Bible and how we got it. Jewish

Women's Archive. "Encyclopedia." jwa.org/encyclopedia, accessed August 29, 2016.

Comprehensive encyclopedia of amazing women.

Mar, Alex. "The Rebel Virgins and Desert Mothers Who Have Been Written Out of Christianity's Early History." *Atlas Obscura* (newsletter), January 21, 2016, http://www.atlasobscura.com /articles/the-rebel-virgins-and-desert-mothers-who-have-been -written-out-of-christianitys-early-history?utm_source=facebook .com&utm_medium=atlas-page .

There are so many fierce women in our religious history who most people don't know about. This is a nice introduction to some of them.

Newsom, Carol A., and Sharon H. Ringe, eds. *Women's Bible Commentary*. Louisville: Westminster John Knox, 1998.

Essays on each book of the Bible with particular attention to the female characters.

Plaskow, Judith. *Standing Again at Sinai: Judaism from a Feminist Perspective*. San Francisco: Harper & Row, 1990.

Plaskow's most influential book and the first Jewish feminist book published. The author is known for her writings particularly on the erasure of women from narrative and history.

Porath, Jason. *Rejected Princesses*, http://www.rejectedprincesses. com, accessed August 29, 2016.

Not specifically about women in the Bible but about all kinds of historical women who were complete bad-asses. Good place to make connections between the Bible and history.

Schüssler Fiorenza, Elisabeth. *In Memory of Her: A Feminist Theological Reconstruction of Christian Origins.* New York: Crossroad, 1983.

> A classic of feminist biblical interpretation.

Trible, Phyllis. *Texts of Terror: Literary-Feminist Readings of Biblical Narratives.* Philadelphia: Fortress Press, 1984.

> Another classic, this one confronting some of the most violent and painful stories in our Bible. Trible is unrelenting in her exploration.

Williams, Delores S. *Sisters in the Wilderness: The Challenge of Womanist God-Talk.* Maryknoll, NY: Orbis, 1993.

> Reading the Bible from a black woman's perspective.

Winner, Lauren F. *Wearing God: Clothing, Laughter, Fire, and Other Overlooked Ways of Meeting God.* New York: HarperOne, 2015.

> Essays on all kinds of imagery for God that is not masculine, much of it having nothing to do with gender at all.

Come to that, anything by Lauren Winner. Or Kathleen Norris or Nadia Bolz-Weber or Debbie Blue or Barbara Brown Taylor or Phyllis Tickle or Rachel Held Evans or Anne Lamott. Really, anything.

Finally, here are a couple of further writings that might be more meta but helpful nonetheless:

Sprinkle, Preston. "What the Bleep Does the Bible Say about Profanity?" *Relevant*, August 22, 2014, http://www.relevantmagazine.com/life/what-bleep-does-bible-say-about-profanity.

> Why swearing is not only okay, it's helpful, particularly when talking about faith life.

Zierman, Addie. "Recovering from Legalism." *Off the Page*, June 29, 2016, http://offthepage.com/2016/06/29/recovering-from-legalism-dear-addie-7.

A blog post about learning to read scripture through a different lens.